# Confessions

## of a Woman
## in Real Estate

And How To Do It Your Way

# Hannah Schuhmann

Published in 2023 by Coaching for Women, Brisbane Australia
www.coachingforwomen.au
Copyright © 2023 Hannah Schuhmann

Title: *Confessions of a Woman in Real Estate -*
      *And How To Do It Your Way*
Author: Hannah Schuhmann

PRINT ISBN: 9780645869606
EPUB ISBN: 9780645869613
Subjects: Women in Business | Real Estate | Professional Development

Book Production Services: www.smartwomenpublish.com

A catalogue record for this
book is available from the
National Library of Australia

NATIONAL
LIBRARY
OF AUSTRALIA

Disclaimer:
The material in this publication is of the nature of general comment
only and does not represent professional advice. All material is provided
for educational purposes only. We recommend to always seek the
advice of a qualified professional before making any decision regarding
personal and business needs. To the maximum extent permitted by
law, the author and publisher disclaim all responsibility and liability
to any person arising directly or indirectly from any person taking
or not taking action based on the information in this publication.

# Contents

# Introduction

Feeling a little emotional, I stood on the balcony of a luxury penthouse apartment near the centre of Brisbane, gazing out over her spectacular riverside City Botanic Gardens and the wide and slow-moving Brisbane River. I was thrilled, having just sold this fabulous property and nearly doubling my seller's original purchase price.

Success! This was my second year of owning my own real estate business and sales were pumping. I worked with an excellent team of staff and consultants, and managed multimillion-dollar monthly sales.

Soon afterwards, I received a Lord Mayors' Multicultural Business Award, one of the initiatives of the Brisbane City Council, supporting business owners in their city. I had received many sales awards before, but this one was special as it recognised me for taking a leap of faith from emigrating to Australia to becoming the boss of my own thriving real estate business.

I was over the moon, and yet it all felt a little surreal. Arriving in Australia 14 years earlier as a German backpacker was a distant memory.

How did I get here from there?

# 1 The Rush is in the Risk

# Chapter One

# Hansa's Early Adventures in Europe

We are all very different individuals, we real estate agents. Diversity is the name of the game. But there are some non-negotiables in our character traits: resilience, honesty, determination and an unquenchable desire to do our very best, whatever happens. Let me tell you the story of how I became an agent. It's a long story – I've been around a few years – so this is your first lesson: resilience pays off.

I grew up in Lohr, a small Bavarian town on the river Main, a chocolate-box setting, complete with a snow-white castle. Raised in a working-class home, my parents worked extremely hard and made sacrifices to provide for me and my four siblings.

My mum realised early on that I was a free spirit, full of energy and at action stations every minute. She nicknamed me 'Hansa' as in the German airline, Lufthansa, as I was always taking off somewhere.

A real terror, I often pushed the boundaries, getting into trouble by injuring myself, my siblings, and my cousins. They still wear the scars of my misadventures.

On my fifth birthday, my parents surprised me with a pink bike. It was the best present ever and I loved it so much. I took it out straight away, with my younger brother on his scooter in tow. After a few trials of learning how to ride it, I fell off. The bike landed on top of me, smashing my left leg.

My 3-year-old brother tried to pull me up, but I could not move. A local woman carried me home. Driving to the doctor in Uncle Adolf's car (yes, that was his name) I did not dare to make a sound, hiding the excruciating pain. I was worried my parents would take my bike away.

The doctor was surprised to see I had multiple leg fractures. I spent over three months in hospital and that killed my modelling aspirations right there. I still have a 25-centimetre scar to prove it. It looks like large teeth marks, and these days it sounds plausible when I say I was attacked by a crocodile.

Leaving hospital, I wasted no time and learned quickly how to walk again. It was painful, yes, but I was bursting to get outside, and I didn't want to miss out on life.

Months later, with my bike accident long forgotten, I told my friend Sylvia we would race our bikes down a steep hill without using brakes. I won the race, but when I looked back, Sylvia was lying on the footpath in tears. She had lost control and hit the kerb. Her knees took the brunt and blood squirted everywhere. Luckily, she was fine.

Both competitive from an early age, one of my cousins had challenged me to a sprint around our yard, with first prize being my favourite Haribo sweets. Halfway, I realised I couldn't catch him, so I threw a tart with perfect precision into his heel. He screamed and stopped instantly. Triumphant, I passed him and won the game—although I had to fight for the lollies afterwards.

This killer instinct of mine to do whatever it takes just took over: it wasn't my fault.

Then, just once, I was responsible for babysitting my younger sister. I pushed her pram a little too forcefully and it accidentally took off down the hill. I watched in horror as the pram bounced off a brick fence. My baby sister and the entire bedding fell out onto the road.

A neighbour had watched the drama unfold and quickly scooped her up and returned her to the pram. She was fine, but I had to suffer through yet another week's house arrest.

When it was summer, we were unsupervised and dreamed up our own games and challenges. My Dad had built an amazing swing in our garden. At least, I thought so. Our house doctor, who visited frequently, called it the gallows, as it was a huge wooden structure, set above a cement path.

I would perform acrobatics and perfect the moves. I challenged my younger brother to follow my lead and replicate them. Regrettably, he came off the swing, landed on his head, and suffered a concussion. The doc was called once again. Luckily for me, my brother still doesn't remember a thing.

School was incredibly challenging for me, particularly when I was young. I feared every single day. I just could not understand the value of sitting still in a classroom on a perfectly fine day. In today's world, I may have been diagnosed with ADHD (attention-deficit/hyperactivity disorder), but that was not a thing then.

The one subject I loved and excelled in was sports. I was thrilled when a higher-level class poached me to play 'voelker ball' for their team. The name loosely translates to 'murder ball'.

Life in our town was governed by the seasons, the catholic church, the soccer club and the 'gesangsverein', the local choral society. The whole town was involved. The perpetual seasonal festivals and club socials were heart-warming and terrific fun and I miss them dearly.

On the flip side, unspoken rules and restrictions had to be obeyed—how to dress, what to say, and in general, how to assimilate. My family would frequently challenge me: 'You're not going to church in that outfit?' or 'That's not how we do things around here'. Blending in is not my strong suit at any time.

I did, however, participate in a traditional dance group and performed to oompah music, dressed in a traditional dirndl. Still, I always felt like an alien. I didn't fit in, and I dreamed of seeing the world.

At 13 years of age, I secretly went to the local phone box, making sure the town gossip, Maria, did not see me. Excited, I called a Frankfurt agency for an au pair job in Hong Kong. All went swimmingly until the recruitment officer asked me whether I had my parent's permission. Caught out, I quickly hung up and was disappointed. I came soooo close.

My adventures did not stop in high school. Sylvia and I skipped school regularly, swapping maths and English classes for Coca-Cola in the local Stern Keller bar. We listened to hard rock, checked out the talent, and had a super time. My much younger brother, now a police officer, would certainly have disapproved of this venue.

To get out of class, I would brazenly go to the head-master's office every other week and tell him that I felt sick. My heart would pound out of my chest when I performed my act. I would nervously plead with him to let me go home early and have Sylvia escort me in case I passed out.

Each time I succeeded, which was every time, I had a huge adrenaline rush. To this day it is a mystery to me why the principal never questioned me. Perhaps he didn't want to be there either.

The end of my second year at high school loomed. My bestie Sylvia and I discussed the prospect of our seriously bad school report cards reaching our parents. Acutely aware of the repercussions we faced, we shook our heads and agreed that there was no way we could go home.

After school the next day, we met up with Gabi, Sylvia's sister, at our home from home, the Stern Keller, and she brought a huge chocolate torte along. It was the best cake I had in my life. We devoured it promptly, without Gabi getting a look in. She could not believe her eyes, and still has not forgiven us.

Hours later, we walked towards the nearby forest: the darkness was unnerving, and it rained heavily. As we reached the edge of town, we heard police sirens approach. Freaked out, we jumped into a soggy field and hid in the scrub. Paranoid, we wondered if they were already searching for us. Now covered in mud, we were looking a little worse for wear. We continued into the woods and bunked down in a small dilapidated wooden shed. We had absolutely no plan.

Our supplies were limited and the couple of nights we stayed in the hut were freezing. Defiantly, we huddled together, getting more and more worried.

Finally, Uncle Bernard, Mum's brother, found us and convinced us to leave the forest and come back home. Gabi had cracked under pressure from our families and disclosed our location. Bernard took us to a pub for a cheerful bratwurst and lemonade, and a debrief on the state of play at home.

That we did not look forward to facing our parents was an understatement. He encouraged me with:

'Come on Hannelore (Hannah). Es wird nichts so heiß gegessen, wie es gekocht wird', meaning 'You never eat the food as hot as it is cooked'. He promised me things would be okay. Everyone needs an Uncle Bernard in their life!

Bernard ran a successful building company. He generously helped my parents with the construction of our family house. He was jovial, loved a party, and was extremely supportive of my mum. Often overwhelmed, she worked night shifts as a waitress and looked after us all during the day. She tirelessly prepared endless meals and sewed all our clothes, which always looked beautiful. Her struggles were painful to watch, and I decided then that I would never have children.

To give my mum a break, Uncle Bernard's family would invite me now and then to their weekender, a Californian bungalow across the river. The property and setting were magnificent, and my siblings were jealous. To me it felt like a punishment: I would be terribly homesick but despite that, it left an impression on me and may have ignited my passion for property and business.

After Uncle Bernard returned me from the forest to my home that day, my mum prepared a hot bath for me. In tears, she hugged me and asked, 'Why did you do that to me?' That broke my heart. As it turned out, Uncle Bernard had been right.

After the dust had settled, I breezed through my education. Almost. First, I had to repeat a school year at a hospitality school for naughty girls. There I was officially the smartest of the dumbest students. Bored out of my brain, I decided to use this as a wake-up call and do better. No way was I going to end up working in a factory for the rest of my life.

There are strict career paths in Germany and once someone has dropped out of school, it is extremely difficult for them to obtain decent well-paid employment.

At the end of the repeated year, my school card had all subjects marked with a 1, the top score in the German school system. (The grades range from 1, the highest, to 6, the lowest.)

That school year, however, was not without drama. I clearly remember a day trip to 'Fraenkische Schweiz', or Franconian Switzerland, a tourist retreat in northern Bavaria.

Ms Elsa Schmitt, an old-fashioned schoolteacher who held me in high regard, accompanied us. After exploring stalagmite caves, we had lunch in a farmhouse. The young owner, a handsome George Clooney look-alike, served us.

Always up for a challenge, I made a bet with my friend Claudia that I would kiss him before lunch finished. As I kissed him, I heard the loudest screech from Ms Schmitt, who pulled me outside. All buffed up, her face bright red with fury, she reprimanded me. I had to sit in the bus and wait for everyone to finish. I felt a bit guilty disappointing Ms Schmitt, but then again, it was so worth it.

I graduated with exceptional results after all, and armed with my newfound worth, I landed a three-year apprenticeship as a chef in a small town called Grossheubach, 65 kilometres from my home.

The restaurant was small, but the head chef was very experienced. His skills had taken him all over the world—five-star hotels in Switzerland, luxury British Cunard cruise liners, and to the French Alsace region, a foodie's paradise.

I was worked extremely hard, which I did not mind. I was acutely aware that this could be my stepping-stone to a career in Switzerland.

I had the role of entremetier, tending to the vegetable and salad station, although the training involved me preparing anything and everything from stroganoff to wild pig roast, to carving up a deer. I gave it my all.

Next time you are eating out, spare a thought for the hardworking chefs enduring the heat and fast-paced environment of a kitchen. Then again, also keep an eye out for any foreign objects, like a temporary crown, in your rice or mushroom sauce... eww... just saying.

As part of my salary package, I lived in staff accommodation onsite. On my days off I would hitchhike back to my hometown, as there were no suitable direct public transport connections.

The first leg of my journey took me to Wertheim, a town with a large American army base. From there, it was another 30 kilometres through the forest to my home.

Hitchhiking was an extremely dangerous pursuit in the early eighties, or, as Ivan Milat proved, really at any time. There were regular news reports of hitchhikers being raped, or worse, killed by American soldiers. I was determined not to let that stop me though: I had a knife.

I would make it a rule to only hitchhike during the day, but one time it was late, and already dark, when I set out. A black Audi with just the driver inside stopped to give me a lift. Usually, I would listen to my gut and if I felt uneasy on approach, I would sometimes tell the driver that I changed my mind, then wait for the next car.

This time I got in, but from the outset this driver was strangely quiet. I could not manage to start a conversation. Half an hour in, he suddenly pulled into a rest area in the middle of the forest.

He switched off the lights, took the keys, and left the car. 'S$%!', I panicked. It was completely dark and unnervingly quiet. I anticipated my passenger door being opened and was on high alert.

Slowly I pulled out my knife from my boot. I held it tight with both hands, ready for action. My heart was racing and after what felt like forever, he opened the driver's door, sat down, switched on the motor, and drove off. I discreetly dropped the knife back into my boot and started to breathe.

I have no idea to this day whether it was an act by a well-meaning man who wanted to scare me into stopping that dangerous activity, or something else. Ignorantly, I continued hitchhiking but listened a little more to my intuition.

During my hitchhiking time, I met lots of fun, compassionate people, too. One Christmas Eve, I tried to make it back home for the celebrations but got stuck on the freeway near a small quiet town, 20 kilometres from home. It was dark and cold, with temperatures below-freezing point, and yes, I broke the rule of daylight-only trips once again. I was bitterly cold and had phoned my parents twice already to check if my brother had come home and could pick me up. No luck.

Deflated, I left the phone booth when a car stopped unexpectantly right next to me. I was surprised, because no one ever leaves the fast-moving freeway to come to this village. It was a town we would label as 'Da liegt der hund begraben' in German, meaning, 'the dog is buried there'—in other words, no one would ever visit.

A Christmas miracle. A happy family was in the car and the wife opened her window and asked, 'Would you know the way to Lohr?' I replied, 'If you give me a lift, I'll show you.' And they did. Was it a coincidence, or an angel to the rescue?

At the end of my apprenticeship, the final exam day arrived. Was I to become a chef? Like a lottery, we picked our exam tasks out of a box. I looked at my ticket in despair: veal rouladen was fine, but a trout cocktaaiiil?

One of the examiners accompanied me into the cellar to a fish tank. I admitted to him that I had never killed a fish before. So, he took the fish out of the tank, killed it with a wooden mallet and handed it to me. No one was any wiser.

Despite butchering the trout cocktail—it really did look like a dog's breakfast—I passed with flying colours. Due to my excellent college grades, I was able to finish my apprenticeship six months early. I like to think that many ice cream rendezvous with my teacher after school had absolutely nothing to do with it.

One of my other college teachers, Norbert, believed I could do more and encouraged me to go back to study and complete a high-school degree. I will be forever grateful to him. I moved back home and enrolled in a Technical College in Hanau, Hessen, just 13 kilometres from my hometown.

It was a difficult one-and-a-half years, to say the least. Some of the high-level maths was killing me, not to mention the English classes. 'I only understood bahnhof' (train station), a German expression meaning, 'I didn't have a clue'. In the end, I passed. Channelling Forest Gump, 'That is all I have to say about that.'

It wasn't all bad though—it was the eighties. What was there not to love—the powerful shoulder pads and tight jeans, which I could only zip up lying on my bed with my younger sister sitting on top of me. I pulled off the big hair styles and was crazy about the music.

My friends and I danced under the bright disco lights to songs like 'Wild Thing, You Make my Heart Sing' by the Troggs; Queen's 'I Want to Break Free'; and 'Total Eclipse of the Heart' by Bonnie Tyler. Oh, please bring back the eighties.

Leaving a disco late one night, I was driving home through the forest, alone in my VW Beetle. A devil in the car, I love to drive fast with the music turned up to full volume.

Speeding along, I recall vividly that suddenly it got unusually hot in the car, and I felt impending danger. The weird thing was, I sensed someone was sitting behind me. Scared, I took courage and touched the backseat, but no one was there. Yet there was this strange presence. Alarmed, I decided to slow down the car and switched off the music.

I turned around a sharp left-hand curve, and there was a large deer standing in the middle of the road, staring at me in the headlights. I was able to easily swerve around it and avoid an accident.

Then, it was serenely calm in the car, and I was completely relaxed. My boyfriend of six months had died a few months earlier, along with several friends, in a car accident on those dangerous roads, and I was convinced his spirit had come to warn me.

\* \* \*

My work resumé started to look good. While the certified chef and the high-school degree qualifications were great, I needed additional accounting and management skills to move into executive positions in

Switzerland, so I applied for another apprenticeship as a Hospitality Accountant in various hotels from the north to the south in Germany.

I scored an interview for a position in a traditional hotel in Garmish-Partenkirchen. Yes, it's not a swear word: it's the name of a skiing town in Bavaria, where the rich and famous come to play. I knew the standard of training would be high, and it would be a fantastic addition to my resumé.

Excited about the interview, I made the long eight-hour journey on the autobahn and some country roads, getting lost a couple of times. Determined to make it, I arrived just in time. The meeting with the insanely good-looking hotel owner lasted just twenty minutes and he told me there and then to join the one-hundred-plus team.

We quickly walked around the hotel; he introduced me to a couple of managers, showed me the bar and five restaurants, and I started within the week. I could not believe my luck.

I didn't realise it then, but the owner calculated that my chef experience would come in handy if the kitchen brigade needed reinforcement, and they would.

The town had a shortage of accommodation, so I ended up in the large hotel roof attic with four other girls. It was cosy, with absolutely no privacy, and it was Party Central, which I did not mind.

It was my first Christmas Eve, 'Heilig Abend', away from home—the time when Germans traditionally celebrate Christmas. We were all homesick and decided to have a huge party in our quarters under the roof. The food and beverage manager was a kind man who supplied us with vast amounts of liquor.

We prepared a 'feuerzangenbowle', which turned out to be deadly, literally. It's a traditional mulled wine, with a sugar cane soaked in rum dripping into the brew, except the wine was mixed with whiskey and schnapps. We had a fabulous, but rowdy time and noisily partied all night.

Unbeknown to us, a couple of floors down, one of the hotel guests suffered a heart attack and died. As a good Catholic girl, I still feel guilty about that night—but not any other nights.

As well as falling madly in love with Karl, one of the chefs, I really enjoyed learning the ropes of hospitality management. I worked in accounts and payroll, and moved through different roles in the restaurants.

I set up a souvenir shop from scratch within the hotel for the famous 'The Oberammergau Passion Play'. It is performed every ten years by the inhabitants of nearby

Oberammergau. Renowned all over the world, it's a regular sell-out, and Garmisch-Partenkirchen is packed with holidaymakers. I would visit picturesque Oberammergau, purchase souvenirs, then sell them for a profit in the hotel shop, mostly to American tourists.

At other times, I would work with public relations. I was asked to host the draw of a competition which offered hotel accommodation and a restaurant package as the prize. Microphone in hand, and under the watchful eyes of a lawyer, the local press, and hundreds of guests, I would draw the prize, entertain the crowd, and promote the hotel.

One New Year's Eve it was all hands on deck. My colleague and friend Suzie, who was highly educated and spoke very eloquently, was to be the witch, entertaining the guests. She would move from table to table and have guests pour hot lead into ice water, creating a silhouette. Suzie would then use this shape to read the guest's future and drink to their good health. She serviced hundreds of tables that night.

When the clock sounded twelve at midnight, I wished all my friends a 'Happy New Year', but where was Suzie?

The next morning, as I walked along one of the hotel corridors I heard a rumble in one of the wooden antique cupboards. Suddenly, the doors opened, and Suzie rolled out onto the floor. She looked terrible.

She had never been more drunk in her life and mistook the cupboard for her bedroom. One thing is for sure—hospitality is a lot of fun.

\* \* \*

The apprenticeship training college was in Munich and, one time, a film crew visited our class. We had to complete a questionnaire on general knowledge about Italy. The top five students were to be selected to be a part of a documentary filmed in Bologna or Modena in Italy. Valentina, my Italian friend, had all the answers and so we worked together and were both invited onto the set.

In Italy, we filmed and dined in various stunning restaurants in Modena and the surrounding vineyards. We visited impressive ceramic workshops and divine cloth factories. Best of all, we test-drove Ferraris at the Ferrari factory in Maranello.

On our return, we were invited to a quiz show in Munich to compete with another team over questions about the culture in Modena and Bologna. I borrowed my boyfriend Karl's frog-green Alpha Romeo Sprint and raced on the autobahn to Munich. I realised I had killed the motor when the car went up in smoke.

I left the car on the side of the super-highway and got a lift the rest of the way, making it onto the show just in time. It was a wonderful experience, apart from the fact that I couldn't stop talking about the food of Italy, as only the Germans know how.

The two and a half years I spent in Garmisch-Parten-kirchen passed quickly. Winter seasons were taken up with skiing when I had free time, followed by obligatory après ski festivities in gorgeous chalets.

During the summer seasons I hiked in the alps and most afternoons the whole team would go swimming nude at the Eibsee, a lake below the Zugspitze, the highest mountain in Germany. Germans take their clothes off anywhere, right?

It was harmless fun, except for Juliette's nipples: they turned into weapons after the swim in the icy water.

When I finished my apprenticeship six months early, I was invited to stay on as an assistant manager. I had completed all qualifications in Hotel Management that a Swiss recruitment manager would expect to see on a resumé. I started to believe in myself.

Feeling confident, Karl and I contacted Swiss employ-ment agencies. He soon scored a sous-chef position, second in charge in the kitchen, in one of the five-star hotels in Zermatt.

"

# Just believe in yourself. Even if you don't, pretend that you do and, at some point, you will.'

–Venus Williams

In June 1985, I was accepted as a 'gouvernante' or assistant manager in a four-star hotel near St Moritz for the summer season. My dream of a career in Swiss hotels was about to become a reality.

A little daunted, I was introduced to a sixty-plus working brigade of Portuguese housekeepers, porters and room maids. I was responsible for the overall smooth operation of the 300-room hotel. In the evening, I would oversee quality control of the food and check in with guests in the ballroom.

On my days off, I would visit my boyfriend, battling three mountain ranges. Always in record time.

I very much wanted to move closer to Karl in Zermatt, and accepted a position as assistant manager in Muerren, a small village in the Bernese Highlands. At an elevation of 1,638 metres above sea level, in winter it could only be reached by a cable car rising vertically from Lauterbrunnen, the town in the valley below.

In the winter season, Muerren was a living postcard—car-free, and a breath-taking place for skiing, après skiing and eating out. Apart from 'sex, alcohol and rock & roll' there was nothing else to do.

I was busy organising functions, chasing occupancy numbers and keeping a check on staff schedules. Despite working long hours, it did not feel like work.

The energy and fresh air on top of the mountain, living in a vibrant village, was something else.

The backdrop of the Swiss Alps lends itself to an abundance of magical moments. At Christmas, I chauffeured guests via electric cart, the only form of transport in town, into the forest.

The black night was lit up by a full moon, twinkling stars showed us the way, and snowflakes gently floated down from the sky—something that only happens at very cold temperatures. It really was that mystical.

We would stop at a cliff with a view over the Lauterbrunnen Valley and the surrounding snow-capped mountains of the Jungfraujoch and Schilthorn. As a surprise for our guests, we organised Christmas carols to ring out of the forest and served hot mulled wine and traditional Christmas cookies.

The window in my staff accommodation in a close-by chalet framed the Eiger north wall, a fairy-tale view, but eerie as well. A group of Japanese climbers had been caught out by a bad storm in late autumn and their bodies were to be recovered in spring when the winter ice had melted. I would often glance at the mountain and feel sad for their poor souls.

Between working the summer and winter seasons in Switzerland, I filled the gaps with language courses.

I booked a two-month French course at Alliance Française in the heart of Paris and stayed in a small hotel nearby. But... by now, you didn't really expect me to go to school in Paris, did you?

Flashback to my job in Muerren: one of the other Swiss managers, Jonas, had won me over with his charm. He invited me for a romantic 'coupe de champagne,' to the Eiffel Tower. But don't worry, he spoke French, and in any case, 'the best way to learn a language is in bed'. Eventually, Jonas pushed me to confess to my boyfriend Karl that I had fallen in love with someone else. I felt evil.

Then another fabulous summer season in Muerren had come and gone and so had my new love, Jonas. He had introduced me to his ultra-conservative parents and as things got serious, I felt spending my whole life in Switzerland would be too restrictive.

San Francisco beckoned, so I was off to study English for two months. But you didn't really expect me to go to school in San Fran either, did you?

My next stop was a winter season as a Director's Assistant in the Hotel Spider in Grindelwald, an Alpine village in south-central Switzerland. One of my duties involved looking after the Michelin-star French restaurant in the hotel. Regrettably, my conversational French was not up to scratch. Neither was writing the daily menu, which always had a few mistakes.

Consequently, I was demoted to the Italian Ristorante. It could have been worse. I was managing about fifteen handsome Italian waiters and it was 'la dolce vita', pure and simple. Besides, who wants escargots when you can have pizza?

When the winter season in Grindelwald finished, I realised that to advance my hospitality career, I needed to complete a two-year Diploma in Hotel Management and moved back to Germany in April 1987.

A few months before my studies started, I filled in a summer season working as a waitress in Konstanz, a city on the beautiful Lake Constance (Bodensee), in southern Germany. The location was stunning but the work conditions, with a chauvinistic father-and-son team were unbearable.

I resigned shortly after starting and drove 1,054 kilometres to the north of Germany to switch to another waitressing job on the island of Sylt, in Schleswig-Holstein. Hardy's wine bar was set in a historic roundhouse and had a certain air about it. It was originally built by a famous spy, Stanley Joseph Grove Spiro, who had a colourful life. He hid in the building during the war but was eventually captured by the Gestapo.

The lavish restaurant had two evening sittings. High pressured, it was survival of the fittest. My colleagues and I would fight politely over glasses and cutlery, which were always in short supply. We would even hide these behind the curtains between the turnover of tables.

The tips were amazing. It was not unusual to finish my shift with 1,500-plus German marks in my pocket. I was well on my way to financing my hospitality degree.

The island of Sylt is known for its nudist culture. During the day, my friend Sabine and I would enjoy the beach. One time, we walked past a hotel guest we knew as a regular in the restaurant. He played table tennis with his partner in the nude. When he recognised us, he waved with his ping pong paddle to greet us. Then he remembered he was nude. Embarrassed, he quickly dropped the bat to cover his private parts. We smiled.

When the season was finished, I moved to Koblenz, a picturesque Roman city where the Rhein and Mosel rivers meet. There was no time to explore this historic place, as I knuckled down to get through the Diploma in Hotel Management. Listening to theoretical blurbs in a class all day, I quickly became bored and started a full-time night job in a Hungarian restaurant on the side.

When I had a two-month break in my studies, I chose to use the time to improve my French. Enthusiastically, I enrolled in a course in Juan-les-Pins on the coast of the French Riviera, next to Antibes. This time, despite the glamour of the nearby glitzy towns of Nice and Monaco calling me, I stuck with it. I can proudly say 'Je parle francais un petit peu' and 'Voulez-vous coucher avec moi, ce soir?' Ha.

I finished my diploma with an average score of '2', which was fine by me, and, in June 1989, received my certificate as 'Staatlich gepruefte Hotelbetriebswirtin' – my Diploma in Hospitality Management. While I felt a real buzz and a sense of achievement, I was realistic. All the certificates in the world would not mean anything unless I took action and made it happen in the real world.

By now, my family was proud of my strength and achievements. One career move at a time, this black sheep had inspired them to come along on the journey and visit all of the fabulous places I had worked in Germany and Switzerland. Thus, I like to think that I have enriched their lives and redeemed myself just a little.

**"**

# You're stronger than you think you are!'

–A.A Milne

# Chapter Two

# Adapting to Australia, 1989 to 1996

I was a free agent again, and I knew the world was my oyster.

Dropping out of school in 1977 had become a fuzzy memory. The ensuing twelve years had given me extensive experience in all things hospitality and the confidence that came with that. To top it all, I had a shiny hospitality diploma. Would I stay in Europe, or travel further afield?

The recruitment officer at The Hilton Hotel Group offered me a one-year management scholarship after I had passed an interview at their head office in Frankfurt. I could take my pick of locations – either Santa Barbara in California, or Chicago, Illinois, in the United States.

It was perfect! The only catch was waiting about three months for my US Green Card before I could transfer. I locked in Santa Barbara and wondered what to do in the meantime.

Feeling adventurous, I liked the idea of a mystery holiday. I closed my eyes, flicked through my Atlas (the world prior to Google maps), stopped at a random page, and voila, my finger touched down on Australia! Without much consideration, I was thrilled to book a seat on a plane to Perth shortly afterward.

Before I left, I stored my limited belongings at my parents' house. I had enough money for a plane ticket and gambled on my brother being able to sell my car, a Golf, to finance my trip. Knowingly, my Mum asked me, 'You're not coming back, are you?' I dismissed it and laughed.

When I arrived in Perth, I was disappointed there was not one kangaroo hopping around the airport. I went sightseeing around Perth and was in awe.

In those days, I did not have a mobile phone. I received a message from home, via the owner of my hostel accommodation, that relieved me. It read, 'Golf has been sold, money transferred, enjoy your trip, your brother K'. I was off backpacking around Australia.

I straight up fell wildly in love with Western Australia's rugged beauty and one special man in it. It all happened on a romantic sailing trip on the Swan River.

I also travelled all the way around Australia in the iconic red Greyhound bus. My heart still skips a beat when I see their buses driving along Brisbane streets. Some of the highlights of my trip were Broome's Cable Beach, kayaking with fresh-water crocodiles in Katherine Gorge, Ayers Rock (now Uluru), Magnetic Island, snorkelling at the Great Barrier Reef, Brisbane, and the long drive back to Perth on the Eyre Highway over the Nullabor Plain.

A whirlwind wedding ensued on my return to Western Australia, and emigrating sealed my fate.

"

# Not taking chances doesn't actually give us more control at all. It just keeps us from getting what we want.'

–F. Diane Barth L.C.S.W

In Perth, I found it painful to find a job. It was easier for me to meet in person because of my accent and my limited understanding of the peculiarities of the local language. Conversations over the phone would quickly turn into 'I beg your pardon?', 'Please repeat', or 'Whaaaat?'

I blamed it on the Aussies, pulling words together, mumbling, or rudely shortening words. I cried with frustration at the struggle to find the kind of work I was capable of, and I tried everything from cleaning to working as a housekeeper at the Hyatt.

Then, finally, I fell on my feet. An Austrian personnel manager recognised my qualifications, and I began managing the catering department, with about sixty junior staff, at the Perth Zoological Gardens.

I thrived there. I organised Savannah Cocktail parties, with the crowd favourite being my own creation of a bright green 'Zulu punch'. I supervised a variety of restaurants and cafés within the gardens, and best of all, the feeding of rice to three gorgeous baby elephants.

I also trained to be a First Aid officer, as part of a response team on site. If there was an accident anywhere within the Zoo, the closest First Aider had to attend. One time, a call came from the picnic lawn—a baby was unresponsive. Thankfully, Margaret, another First

Aid officer, who was far more experienced than me, assisted.

Another time when I was on my own, a zookeeper was attacked by a pack of spotted hyenas and the call came in over the speakers. Oh my god! I was nervous and raced to the scene with my electric cart. The 'carcass', I mean Russell, was lying outside the enclosure, bleeding from the bum, with his pants ripped to shreds. I rolled him on his side to dress his wounds (… eww) and keep him quiet until the ambulance arrived. But, all the while, to my embarrassment, he kept shouting, 'Hannah, shut up!'

Communicating in English was still difficult for me, and I resorted to sign language. So did my Zoo staff kids. I managed them with an iron fist. Now and then, I would catch them placing their left index finger across under their nose and raising their right arm in salute.

Despite that, parents regularly came to see me and personally thank me for the positive behavioural changes I had effected in their child. One of the boys was now making his bed and tidying his room, his mother told me. (I am sure some of those juniors are still receiving counselling, though.)

At the same time, my husband tried his hand at residential real estate. It soon became clear that a suit and a real estate licence did not guarantee sales. You just can't buy experience or know-how as a newbie in the industry!

The prerequisites for newcomers, apart from having an excellent mentor, are great people skills, charisma, and uber resilience—a never-give-up attitude is essential.

Anecdotal evidence suggests that circa 80 percent of property agents drop out of the industry in their first six months, and only about 10 percent make it past year one, with approximately 5 percent persisting more than five years.

To become a successful real estate agent, it takes grit, off-the-chart work ethics, boundless energy, a love for people and an aptitude for listening. I was confident I had all those skills and thought 'I would love to do that; I would be good at it'.

My husband, Jack, was born in Queensland and he wanted to move back to his home state. We decided to sell our property and pack up our lives in Perth. I realised I was not too bad at sales when, in 1995, I sold our house privately. It had been on the market for months, first with a local agency and then through me via 'Sale by Owner'. "

"

# Our greatest weakness lies in giving up. The most certain way to succeed is always to try just one more time.'

–Thomas Edison

One Saturday, I decided to do some market research and check out my competition. I visited several open houses in the neighbourhood. At one property, I started chatting to a buyer called Cheryl. She started telling me what she didn't like about the house we were viewing. I listened intently as she described what she was looking for.

Enthusiastically, I said, 'That sounds like my place. Why don't you have a look? It is just around the corner.' Incredibly, I sold it to her that day.

I was not a real estate agent then, but, in hindsight, snatching that buyer was a little naughty.

It still amazes me that new agents sell properties quickly, early on in their careers. It is called 'beginner's luck,' or 'ultra-enthusiasm', which is infectious. Exceptional agents maintain that level of energy throughout their careers.

When I sold our house in Perth, the property market was slow due to a building boom and high interest rates that had run for years and created a buyers' market. Still, I made a 50 percent profit in four years of holding that property. Astonishingly, in 2022, it would be worth seven times the value of the original price in 1991.

Inspired by my successful house sale, I began to dream of becoming a real estate agent. I decided to make it a reality when we moved to Brisbane.

After moving there, I had to come to terms with being in an unhealthy relationship. Jack had issues. He had physically abused me. I am at loss now as to why I had let him get away with it for over five years.

When I left Germany, my dad said something to me which sounded strange at the time: 'If things get tough, stick with your man'. It turned out to be, without a doubt, the worst advice I received in my life.

In Perth, I once went with a friend to a Tina Turner concert. An awesome performer, at the end of the evening she pointed the microphone into the crowd and asked women to roar. A huge thundering sound shook the hall.

Then she probed, 'Now let's hear it from the men', and there were only a few scattered cheers. Tina then screamed at the top of her lungs, 'Should we give them another chance?' She paused and whispered, 'We always do!' The audience went berserk.

There was no reasoning with Jack. One time after a party, he got very drunk and attacked me violently. I was lying on a footpath, humiliated, thinking I would die right there. But I didn't.

Then my passport disappeared. I went through physical and emotional warfare.

I had a split personality about the situation. One part of me loved him. And I couldn't begin to think that I'd failed at emigrating to Australia. The other part of me was screaming to find a way out. I had no one to confide in, and I would have felt too ashamed to, anyway.

I kept up the charade of a happy life with work colleagues, my family in Germany, and friends, as most abused women did at that time. It was long before the #MeToo movement, and there was very little protection for female emigrants.

Once in Brisbane, I mustered up all my courage and said my goodbyes to Jack. I didn't see myself as a victim. I was determined not to be defined by it. I forgave myself for not acting sooner, and I forgave Jack for being weak and not finding the strength to repair the damage done by his poor upbringing.

Did I learn my lesson? Of course not! But it sure taught me perseverance and how to break through the pain barrier, both invaluable traits for a real estate agent.

I was ready for my next adventure in tropical Queensland. '*What's loooooove got ta do with it! Whaaaat's loooove got ta do with it?*' I was free again!

"

Sometimes you've got to let everything go——purge yourself. If you are unhappy with anything ... whatever is bringing you down, get rid of it. Because you'll find that when you're free, your true creativity, your true self comes out.'

–Tina Turner

# 2
# Hannah's 5 KEYS to Real Estate Success

# Chapter Three

# Getting Serious about Success

My career spanning 20+ years in real estate lifted me to remarkable heights and occasionally dropped me to absolute hellish despair. I survived dramas and tantrums, battled buyers' finance troubles and my own cash flow challenges. I enjoyed awesome sales successes, whilst navigating ever-changing property cycles and male-dominated industry politics.

Uber passionate about the work I do, I relish dealing with people and always have their best interests at heart. Granted, that did not apply to everyone. I ignored two-faced agents and their unethical behaviour. In the property jungle, there is the ever-present danger of being pulled over to the dark side by association. This may sound harsh, but trust me, I'm a Real Estate Agent.

Starting in real estate is like trying to make it big in Hollywood. Not everyone succeeds, but anyone can copy someone who has worked it out!

The real estate world is high-paced, fun, super competitive, and has a never-ending steep learning curve. Let's get you ahead of the game. Ready, set, action! Come along on the ride and realise your burning real estate aspirations with what I believe to be the five keys to a successful career in property.

Not dissimilar to my life, which has rarely travelled in a linear way, the stories are not in chronological order and are placed to best reflect the five keys to success in this industry:

Key 1: Establish your POSITION in the industry
Key 2: Let your PASSION show
Key 3: Connect with your PEOPLE
Key 4: The PRICE matters – but it's not everything
Key 5: The subtle art of the PUSH

# KEY ONE

---

## Establish your POSITION in the Industry

# Chapter Four

# Positioning — YOU

In a proud moment in 1997, I held a Real Estate Sales Certificate from the Real Estate Institute of Queensland (REIQ) in my hands and was itching to launch my property career.

Determined to succeed, I applied for positions in residential offices in the Western Suburbs of Brisbane in Queensland. It was one of the red-hot areas in the 90s, and best of all, I was living there.

Positioning yourself within an advantageous area is imperative in real estate, even in today's high-tech world. Of course, you can live in and reach the top in any area.

I accepted a sales role in a prominent real estate office and dealt with the basics of arranging Professional Indemnity Insurance (a must-have 'get out of jail card' you hope you will never have to use). A clean car and business attire were expected. And so was the latest mobile phone—a compact Nokia the size of a house brick. I ticked all the boxes. I was ready ... or so I thought.

## Positive mindset

Call me naïve, but, innately, I always expect the best in life. Starting out in real estate was no different. Optimistic and beyond excited, I was ready to jump right in and I trusted that I would be fine. You do really want someone to believe in you—especially you.

I was confident that I would succeed and totally believed that I could make it. Strong-minded, there was not a doubt in my mind that I would find a way to make it happen. Are you not convinced about your own success? Just 'fake it till you make it'. Clients are acutely aware of your mental attitude: the way you see yourself is the way the rest of the world will see you.

People fascinate me. Ever curious, I want to know everything about them. An interrogation (in a nice way) often ensues when I meet someone new. My enthusiasm is real, and so is treating everyone I meet like family or friends. Why waste precious moments when there is an opportunity to be happy with the people you're with? You have got to be passionate as a real estate agent. Your positive mindset and optimism will be irresistible.

Keep your mind sharp and prioritise your happy place—and I'm not talking drugs here. Anecdotal evidence suggests that some agents power through their days high on designer drugs to cope with the stress of the industry. If you want longevity in property, face your daemons and learn to be high on life.

My philosophy in life is to combine any tedious but necessary task with something pleasurable. I would do those pesky but important weekly feedback letters to my sellers from a nice café on the river. Or listen to relaxing music whilst drawing up a contract.

To stay at the top of my game, I stay physically fit, and healthy rituals are important to me. Daily, weekly, and three-monthly routines help me to stay balanced and focused and keep my performance at the highest possible level.

My favourites are meditations, qigong, Pilates, boot camps, weekly acupuncture sessions, massages, travel, and anything 'Eat, Dance, Love'. I strongly recommend investing in yourself: you are your greatest resource.

Psychological strength will be invaluable in challenging meetings with prospective sellers, handling the constant stream of buyer enquiries, and dealing with the relentless cycle of the highs and lows in a demanding sales environment.

It's also a great advantage when you encounter the male 'alpha agents'. Believe me, they are out there and ready to suck your life force right out of you. These types of agents will try to dominate, intimidate, and rattle your cage.

I deal with them with my own self-talk: 'Stand your ground. Smile and embrace your self-worth.' And something I learned from Justin Herald: 'I don't care how good you are, I am better!'

Do not fall into the trap of mimicking the aggressive agent demeanour either. Instead, make it a goal to leave your clients, and everyone else you meet, happier than they were before meeting with you. It will accelerate your career.

## First day

It was Monday morning, my first day in the office. What now? I was looking for a friendly face. As all the agents streamed into the office, it was clear that I may have been the only female amongst the salespeople. By now, having lived in Australia for a few years, I was aware that there was an invisible, unspoken divide between women and men. I had seen it around barbeques, at social gatherings, and in corporate environments.

Larry, another agent, arrived and was sitting directly behind me, our chairs almost touching. He grunted a quick 'Good morning' and proceeded to unlock the padlock securing a huge chain wrapped around his filing cabinet! 'Interesting … what the hell?' I thought.

I learned later that he was protecting his leads. Larry was not going to share his energy and time with a newcomer like me. I didn't really blame him. His face revealed what he was thinking: 'Will she stay, or will she go?'

I pondered whether I had picked the right office. Well, I had no choice: it was the only agency that gave me a shot, after unsuccessful interviews with other offices in the area. One company that had arranged three interviews with me, then rejected me, eventually became my main competition. They later nicknamed me 'the Schumanator'. Nice!

## Sales meeting

But back to my first day in property. Heath, the sales manager, invited me to the Monday morning compulsory sales meeting. All agents, sales managers, and directors were squashed together in the boardroom. The tension was palpable, the air electrifying and there was nowhere to hide.

One of the company directors painstakingly discussed sales targets and open house results from the weekend. Then the agents were scrutinised. All looking serious, they reported their successes... or none.

*How many 'For Sale' signs are up, compared to your competitors? How many offers and/or contracts were signed? How many listings are in the pipeline? When are you closing the various deals?*

Some sellers had reduced their sales prices. The listing agents were praised for 'putting on the thumbscrews', to 'condition the seller'—I mean, managing to inform the seller of the real market price. The team was encouraged to reconsider showing stale listings to any prospective buyers.

Things got heated easily. There were lots of 'Show me the money' moments. Think 'Jerry Maguire': Why, for God's sake, was a deal not closed when the difference in price was minimal? Who had the right over a certain buyer? Did X encroach on someone's BDA (business development area); and how about that one-sided commission split between the selling and buying agents … and so on.

When the session was finished, everyone rushed out like the room was on fire, motivated to achieve better results by next week. Or at least that's what it looked like: the pressure was on.

In time, I learned to adapt to the high-powered Monday morning meetups. I tailored my responses creatively, presenting my ambitious sales pipeline, and then paddled like crazy to get there by the following week.

There was a running joke in the office that a 'Let's have a coffee' invitation from Heath after the Monday morning's meeting would most certainly mean, 'It's all over, Red Rover.' In fact, Heath would regularly ask one of the agents for coffee, and we all knew the significance.

One thing was crystal clear—coffee with the sales manager was to be avoided at any cost. I decided to stay super focused on learning how to list properties. My aim was to, at the very least, cover the associated expenses for my desk set-up, and make a profit for the office, so ensuring my survival. Simple.

Game on, with absolutely no clue and a German accent! It turned out the accent would be an advantage.

"

# Success is often achieved by those who don't know that failure is inevitable.'

– Coco Chanel

## Real estate caravan

Following the sales meeting, we all attended the somewhat more relaxed 'real estate caravan'. Agents would excitedly take the team to their newly listed properties. It's a 'showing method' where a team of real estate agents visit a property at the start of the marketing. The sellers are suitably impressed when a force of 15+ agents view and compliment the property, and, of course, proclaim, 'We have buyers!'

This was done mainly to give sellers confidence that they had made the right decision in engaging our office but it also gave the agent feedback on the new listing and it was a good exercise for the team to keep abreast of the market.

Typically, a listing agent would view a new property through rose-tinted glasses. This reality check on the way back to the office was a valuable corrective. Colleagues—ok, all of us—took great pleasure in making fun of the quirky aspects of the property. 'What about the purple paint in the master bedroom? The nude artwork in the living area? The odd sculptured letterbox? Asbestos roof, bikie neighbours, one of the sellers in his pyjamas?' ... and so on.

Still, on the way back to the office, we were all scanning our list of buyers in our heads, trying to match them to any of the new listings. Most recently, my database of buyers was quickly accessed in the cloud and came with me wherever I went. Buyer entries were categorised by price range and requirements, which made it much easier to stay in touch.

As a rule, agents protect their listings fiercely and push to sell these fast to collect 100% of the commission. I was no different!

Call me cynical, but to me, the myth that larger companies are more effective due to more agents working together for a successful sale is questionable. Only very few offices, perhaps some with more equitable commission structures, work as a team.

### Business Development Area (BDA)

Heath allocated me my very own BDA. Another agent had just left, and I was thinking briefly, why?

Never mind. I could exclusively 'farm' three suburbs, and one of them happened to be right where I lived. Farming meant I could market myself, and list and sell properties in my BDA.

We were all protecting our areas, fighting tooth and nail to prevent losing listings to other agents within the office.

Occasionally, I would caution my colleagues when I spotted them near my BDA, but they would  mutter defensively that they had just picked up their kids from school. I remember threatening one agent with squeezing a certain part of his anatomy if I caught him again.

Working side by side with mostly men had rubbed off on me and I had become a little hard-mouthed. As a woman in a male environment, I felt I had to become tough to succeed. In hindsight, I could have saved a lot of energy and been true to my values. I could have done all I achieved and more by making good decisions through intuition and creativity.

'Positioning' has become a buzzword in business, and it doesn't just apply to products. I believe it's especially important to reside in, and position yourself in, your BDA. To live and breathe an area has huge advantages. It helps you save time and energy and increases your productivity. This results in better long-term performance, due to the economy of scale and its resulting cost advantages and efficiencies.

Unless you live in the suburb you're selling in, you won't know the specifics of those micro markets. That's why sellers often know the local market better than a real estate agent.

One of my colleagues, Paula, had repeatedly been the absolute top-performing agent in a different fringe area of Brisbane to mine. She had lived and established herself there. When she left, she found it difficult to make inroads in this highly competitive and new environment, the Western Suburbs. She ultimately left the industry. (Although, she could use the people skills learned in real estate in her next career as a psychologist.)

A year after starting my own business, I began specialising in inner city apartments. I then relocated my business from the western suburbs to the Brisbane central business district (CBD), and was amazed by the positive impact it had, and the ease of doing business. I could travel within minutes to inspections and accommodate any spontaneous buyer appointments.

Sometimes interstate clients would phone me to arrange an inspection at short notice. 'When can we see this property? We are going back to Sydney this afternoon?' My response: 'NOW! I will see you in ten minutes!'

Do not think twice about leaving the office: showing properties to purchasers takes top priority over administrative work.

Routinely, I arranged to show other city apartments similar to the one the buyers asked to see, in the same appointment. The reality is that less than 5% of showings result in a sale. Even so, it is imperative to establish strong relationships and provide as much information as possible. I prepared brochures with specific details for each property, as well as educational flyers to supplement verbal discussions around buyers' questions. Topics included the function of a body corporate, depreciation, finance, auction pitfalls, first home buyer rules, legal tips, property myths, and the like.

I delighted in greeting my clients with delicious Swiss chocolates. This made appointments much more fun, and inspired trust and a feeling of connection.

Even if clients didn't purchase through me, they frequently referred me to their friends or returned to sell a property with me years later. They would say, 'We didn't buy through you, but we remember your professional non-pushy approach and we liked dealing with you.'

The key is to provide excellent service, comprehensive information, and quality chocolates. The emphasis here is quality: it might sound banal, but the devil is in the details, from chocolates to contracts. Some competitors have tried to emulate me with cheap chocolate gold coins. Not a good idea.

Because I specialised solely in the city apartment market, I could use advertising monies very effectively and focus thoroughly on service, rather than cutting appointments and client contact short because of travel time.

## Letterbox drops and daily activities

There were a few ways of picking up listings as a newcomer. One was to make calls using the office database. That can be a little tricky, as it's easy to inadvertently step on other agents' toes.

It's a challenging exercise with lots of rejections. But I always pushed through the pain barrier and reached my set goal of calls. If the number was 100, I would phone 100. This resulted in a few leads and connections. I diligently diarised the follow-up and actioned what I promised.

At the start of an agent's career, a fair amount of elbow grease is needed to get established. In addition to the office database, letter box drops and the list of withdrawn properties are also good sources for contacts. Sellers withdraw properties for all sorts of reasons. They may have had a bad experience with the first agent and still want to sell. Their accountant may have advised to delay the sale to the next financial year, or other health or family issues may have popped up.

Staying close to these prospective sellers and providing support and information along the way will lead to listings in the long run.

Some agents unashamedly 'jump signs' as a fourth option. It's an unethical practice where a competitor notices a For Sale sign, then contacts the seller under the pretence that they have buyers, offers or better marketing to get the job done. The REIQ's best practice policy stipulates that an outside agent can't contact a seller during an exclusive Form 6 sales agreement between that seller and their current agent, generally signed for 90 days.

I developed a schedule of daily, weekly, and monthly activities, arranging mailouts to owners of withdrawn properties and database clients, making a certain number of phone calls, producing and posting general mailouts, and arranging leaflet distribution. I would not leave the office in the evening until I finished the tasks in my diary.

Being disciplined, most mornings before going to the office, I diligently distributed my promotional flyers with the aim of contacting each property in my BDA area at least four times in the year.

During these walks, I kept one eye out for annoyed residents jumping from behind bushes and the other for guard dogs waking the neighbourhood.

I was acutely aware that this practice is a pet hate for homeowners. No one liked the constant bombardment of marketing flyers, but it became a little more tolerable for people as they started to think about moving. Of course, until that time, a lot of trees got cut down to supply the paper, as then the average period for a property to be held between sales was seven years.

Despite feeling mischievous as I stuffed my brochures into the already overflowing boxes, I wanted to be in the mix to be considered as their agent when they did finally decide to sell.

Whilst I approached the letterbox drops with trepidation, most established agents would employ companies to deliver the brochures for them, arguing it's a better method for using time more efficiently. I, on the other hand, enjoyed being out and about and getting to know my BDA, and keeping my limited budget in check.

A lot of the locals enjoyed a chat and became familiar with me. They told me everything that was going on in the neighbourhood. 'Oh, see Mrs Hunter down the road—they are looking to buy a unit for their daughter', or 'Did you see Robyn in that white house? I believe she is moving south'.

I would hand out my business cards and ask politely whether they could refer me to the neighbour.

Two months in from starting my career, I walked along an exclusive avenue and noticed a lady outside a house with a lovely garden. I waved and smiled and started chatting with her.

As it turned out, Jenny was visiting from New Zealand. We had a lovely conversation. There was even a connection to Germany between us. I listened to her telling me that her aunt had passed away recently. She was only here for a few days and needed help with selling the property.

I could not believe my luck, and flushed with excitement, I offered, of course, first my condolences, and then, enthusiastically, my help with the presentation of the house and any additional chores which might need organising.

A few days later, Jenny decided to engage me as her selling agent. We had clicked! She was impressed by my passion and by my early morning enthusiasm. She also appreciated the additional service I had offered. She felt we were on the same page.

"

# I feel that luck is preparation meeting opportunity.'

– Oprah Winfrey

Like attracts like. Research by psychologists has found that it's a myth that opposites attract. People who agree with us and display the same attitudes and values feel connected, while disagreements on beliefs create negative feelings and a seller may look for another agent they better align with.

I was ecstatic about my new listing: it was a fabulous residence and suitably admired by the team. The risk of having to share my commission with my colleagues was high. They were promptly hitting the phones to their buyers, so I made sure I sold this popular property without delay. I was on my way!

Unsurprisingly, approximately 80% of sales are transacted by the listing agent and about 20%, if that, by conjunction with another salesperson. A 'conjunction' means a negotiated split of the commission, shared between the listing agent and the selling agent who introduced the buyer to the property.

## Listing agent or 'networker'

There are generally two types of residential sales agents: one focuses on listing properties, and the other type, the 'networkers', are 'running' buyers. These salespeople dance about like blue-arsed flies all over the place, showing properties that are listed within the office, or with other local agents, or are off-market.

All jokes aside, 'networkers' can do well if they have the knack to match buyers with the right properties. This demands huge patience, and years of experience as a listing agent. I used to work with such an operator.

Lyn was softly spoken, and her smile and calm demeanour would instantly inspire trust. She genuinely had a passion for helping buyers to find the perfect property. Whether it was a family home, a development site or a riverfront unit, she was on to it.

She quietly worked away in the background and strategised movements like in the game of Monopoly. For example, she would search tirelessly for a lovely apartment on the river for Elizabeth to purchase, so an off-market purchaser, builder Joe, could build his dream house for his family on Elizabeth's former block of land. Lyn used her intuition and extensive network to produce consistently awesome sales results. She was a unicorn.

Most networkers just don't have enough experience or contacts, and don't know the market well enough to succeed at Lyn's level. There is considerable uncertainty for the networker agent, as frequently the buyer finds their ideal property with another agent. In general, the listing agent protects specifics on price and conditions for the contract, if they have another interested party.

The other gamble is that the buyer's preferred property may be sold before the offer is made, or worse, the buyer goes directly to the listing agent.

On another note, a suitable client-friendly car is a necessity. However, as I was dealing mostly with investors within the compact area of the Brisbane CBD, it was less important to me at the time. I drove a bright lime green Saab convertible with very little legroom in the backseats, which wasn't very practical.

I would avoid taking more than one client in my car. There was one time, however, that I did give a couple of brothers a lift. Unfortunately, the one that was slightly overweight slipped into the back seat. I immediately thought, 'Here's trouble—he will never get out of there'.

When we arrived back at their office, he was indeed stuck between the seats and could not move. His brother held onto both of his hands and tried to pull him out of the car, to no avail. After a while, always practical, I placed both of my hands on his butt and pushed him out of the car. Who says real estate agents don't get their hands dirty?

Not surprisingly, I liked the idea of being a listing agent and in control of the sale and getting paid 90% of the time. A fact of life is that not all properties will sell. There are too many reasons to cover in detail—the seller's price expectation; the property is used as equity for another investment and can't be sold; the property is listed with another agent after expiration of exclusive listing; or sellers change their mind and withdraw the property from sale altogether. It does happen, so get over it. It's part of the numbers game. Next!

The message is loud and clear—if you wish to be in charge of your destiny, focus on becoming a champion listing agent.

Once I sold a house, I would visit the letterboxes again with my success story, with the exception of 'no junk mail' boxes. This kind of marketing would regularly result in potential sellers contacting me to either request a market appraisal, subscribe to my database, or scream their complaints into my ears.

Some agents would use excuses if they received complaints about their flyers. For example, they might say that a distribution company used delivery people with disabilities who didn't notice the 'No Junk' sign on the letterbox. Terrible! I couldn't possibly use that line and I always fessed up.

Today, social media platforms add to the mix to relay successes and newsworthy content. Correctly done, this marketing method can work well if your audience finds your content interesting and if you have the right followers.

# Champions are champions not because they do anything extraordinary but because they do the ordinary things better than anyone else.'

– Chuck Noll (Football Coach)

Don't forget to send thank-you cards and gifts to the buyer, seller, and any referrer. Yes, you might think it's a thing of the past and obsolete in our digitally connected world, but anecdotal evidence from my clients tells me that it is another way to show your human touch and gratitude. A powerful message will mean people remember you and refer you on to their friends.

## Sphere of influence

Starting out, there had been one big factor missing for me. I did not have a 'sphere of influence'. I didn't know anyone: I had no connections; not many friends or affiliates; and not even a supporting partner who could provide emotional and monetary support. I ignored the fact that it takes six to twelve months to become established.

In my BDA I was competing with several well-known female agents. They were highly styled and equally successful, and most were married to husbands with huge connections. They had extensive networks of business associates, neighbours, school, and golf friends.

I had none of that. I knew no one.

I remember thinking, 'How can I compete and what can I offer my clients to compel them to list with me, rather than with my rivals?' The reality is, newcomers

generally do well due to their fresh approach, enthusiasm and genuine, trustworthy demeanour. I realised
people liked dealing with me and I kept moving!

On my daily drive to and from the office, I would keep
my eyes peeled for any changes and take notes. Rental
or sales signs would go up or come down. Houses being
painted, renovated, or gardens freshened up, are all
sure-fire signs that an owner may be thinking of selling.

After starting out in that first real estate office, one of
the company directors annoyingly kept asking me in
passing, 'Are you winning'? Twelve months in, I smiled
and responded with an almost 100% resounding 'Yes'.

It did not happen overnight, but as I became more
experienced, I had built a network in my BDA, and a
solid reputation. Sometimes I would even be entrusted
to sell their own properties for agents who worked for
different property companies in other areas. They
did not use their own franchise, perhaps for privacy
reasons or otherwise. This always surprised me, but I
was equally thrilled.

## What is your trademark? Your point of difference?

If you want to be noticed in a sea of agents, have a point
of difference! What is your secret weapon? Mine is my
German accent, a great conversation starter. It's lovely
when I phone existing clients on my database, and I

don't even need to say my name. Frequently I receive a response straight up with 'Oh yes, Hannah, how are you?' People easily remember me and associate the German side of me with high work ethics and reliability.

Some agents do the trademark thing badly, with tacky marketing and standing out for all the wrong reasons. You know the ones in Superman costumes or silly hats. Other real estate agents wear colourful outfits, drive Ferraris, or have quirky traits—and that's fine if it works for the niche of the property market they are in.

A few could be more-than-friendly with their clients—but not me! Although, over the years, I have had a few encounters. A building manager once tried to kiss me while his wife was in another room only meters away. I was so surprised, all I could hiss was, 'I don't do that!' and rushed out of the unit.

Another time, a purchaser with a foot fetish, who attended my open house, was staring at my feet for the whole duration of the inspection, with various other buyers in attendance. It took me ages to get rid of him.

Some buyers have followed me for months from open house to open house and even brought along romantic picnics. I can't recall how often I have been asked out on a date by clients. It's tricky to let customers down gently without compromising a deal. A smile helps.

For peace of mind, it's a good idea that female agents let someone know where they are going, when appointments are scheduled in the evening, or when feeling unsure about a meeting with a client.

Digital technology can enhance your brand awareness and is complementing and overtaking traditional face-to-face interactions. Social media has become a popular marketing tool and if used correctly, can positively grow your reputation, profile and network. Time-poor agents are already swamped by everyday business requirements, though, so adding posting, blogging, and tweeting can be overwhelming. Therefore, pick your weapon. Consistency is the key here. Learn which medium works best for you. Schedule informative content for your subscribers. Outsourcing social media may also be a good option, if you're prepared to take the cream off the top of your income.

Twelve months into my career, I looked back on my progress. I loved the lifestyle. There had also been lots of late nights with endless phone calls to prospective buyers and sellers; thousands of rejections; hundreds of kilometres of letterbox drops; lots of signs hammered into the ground; and endless dialogues with my more experienced colleagues and superiors. I had consistently hit my sales targets and even won some company awards. I now proudly listed some of the properties which used to be won by the more established agents in my BDA area and started receiving referrals on a regular basis. I was finally winning!

## Mr Bigg

I was on a roll. Things started to happen on a private note as well, I met my new love… sorry, this time I won't kiss and tell, but let's call him 'Mr Bigg'.

He was working in sales as well. This was awesome as he understood the dynamics of the business and was a great sounding board when it came to tricky negotiations. I even roped him in, excuse the pun, to complete a real estate sales certificate.

I remember one time he kindly supported me with an open house. Being a successful sales executive himself in another industry, he was undoubtedly the most overqualified assistant I had ever employed.

His job was to usher buyers into a high-rise building. A couple, Mark and Karen, who attended the open house, turned out to be his friends. Mr Bigg was under strict instructions: 'Don't think for yourself. Do as I tell you, and don't talk to the buyers beyond pleasantries.'

This was important for several reasons. Firstly, a novice can disclose too much and potentially jeopardise a sale. The smallest wrong remark can put doubts in a buyer's mind and muddy the waters.

Secondly, the selling agent needs to establish rapport with the buyer. Two people chatting to them means less time for the buyer to talk, connect, and feel comfortable. Once trust is established, the purchaser will have the confidence to sign on the dotted line.

Thirdly, the agent must always be in control and call the shots, while the assistant is simply the cheerleader. Okay, I know what you're thinking … 'She's a control freak!' That is fine … research shows that people with that personality trait are results-driven, good problem solvers, and natural leaders.

Things went well with Mr Bigg's friends, and they did buy the property.

# Chapter Five

# Positioning — Office

Choosing the right real estate company and office to work with is very important, because it can make or break your career. So, how do you know which office is best? A good place to start is attending various career nights with major franchises. These will provide you with a basic introduction to real estate. Typically, attendees will leave information sessions feeling excited, with a warm fuzzy feeling about the industry.

Another option is to visit real estate offices, chat with sales managers and get a feel for different environments, the company's values, and their guiding principles. Does the agency have a good name? Which office aligns most with your beliefs and feels the most supportive? Attend open houses and annoy agents... I mean, quiz them about their experiences.

Recently, I spoke to a couple of my real estate friends about my book. Interestingly, both suggested I add to watch out for directors who also sell properties rather than just manage the agency, as they may snaffle up the best leads that come into the office.

## Work as personal assistant

Currently, newcomers can start out as a personal assistant to a lead agent for a certain period. A word of warning—ensure that the company you pick has a good reputation, and most importantly, that you share the same moral principles and values with the agent you're working with. Otherwise, you may be burned in the first few months and leave the industry. It could become a punishing period in your life, or worse, you too could be pushed over to the dark side.

## Telemarketing

Then there are some offices that make newbies carry out telemarketing calls for months and months, often with the intention of providing leads to the more established agents. This is a grinding, highly challenging experience to really test the resolve and determination of the most resilient candidates. It is tough, monotonous work, but roll with it: it's a step closer to the goal of selling properties.

Incidentally, in my first year in real estate, I supplemented my income by taking on a telemarketing position with a charity to survive financially. My success in real estate was all that mattered, and I would have done almost anything. I didn't mind working harder to achieve that goal.

The nearly six-month telemarketing interlude was with the RSL (Returned Services League), and it was entertaining for myself, my colleagues, and customers alike. Making the calls with my German accent was a little ironic. Some people answered the phone in disbelief and thought it was a practical joke. The conversations would always end in laughter and a few ticket booklets sold. I saw it as a great learning experience.

On reflection, it was very good practice for cold calling in real estate too—a technique where a salesperson reaches out to potential sellers who have never interacted with you or the office before.

## Mentoring

Another critical support when starting a career in property, or any industry for that matter, is a relationship with a mentor, someone to lean on and who will share their knowledge and experience freely. After all, you can't buy experience. Research shows that experiential learning happens by hands-on doing. Invest the time, then reflect on what went well and what could be improved upon.

In that first office, I was lucky. Heath, the sales manager, was very encouraging: he believed in me and I could not have asked for a better or more experienced mentor. His calm demeanour and wealth of on-tap knowledge got me into the swing of things quickly.

It was a far cry from my previous life in hospitality in Europe where some of my mentors had choleric personalities. Testosterone ruled, and I witnessed frying pans crashing through restaurant windows, and knives flying at staff through kitchens—all in the hope of improving their performance.

Heath was focused on my success as much as I was, and helped me to set my goals. How much did I want to earn per year? We worked back from there. Call or speak with circa X hundreds of people per week. Conduct X appointments and prepare X number of market appraisals. Consequently, list X number of properties to achieve the set sales levels. Easy! It was a numbers game! I liked it.

I thought the goals were achievable and I was clear on how to accomplish them. I now had a plan and a target to aim for. Then I set my sales numbers a little higher, so I would push harder to reach them.

I learned quickly that new agents had approximately three months to make it happen, otherwise it would be curtains and a cup of coffee with Heath.

## Cashflow

Limited cashflow between commissions puts additional pressure on salespeople. It's easier to start off with a safety net of, say, $30,000-plus in the bank to bridge the gap between making the sales to the settlement, when you finally get paid.

Today, real estate offices will pay a minimum wage, which helps. A supportive partner is not only a bonus, but also a non-negotiable if you are in a relationship. Staying on top of your finances is imperative. You don't want to be in a position where you're tempted to compromise your ethics for a sale and destroy your reputation for the sake of financial survival.

A simple excel spreadsheet, budget app, and software tools all help to stay in control of your financial situation.

Did I have cash reserves? Of course not! It was do-or-die for me at the start!

## Team building

We were trekking through steamy dense rainforest on the Sunshine Coast, being pushed forward by a couple of ex-Special Forces guys, when 'Arrgghhhh'...we heard a loud screech from a heavyweight colleague. He had slipped on wet rocks near the top of a steep waterfall. Three of us desperately gripped his arms and legs to save him from falling over a cliff. We joked later that it was lucky he didn't work in sales, otherwise we would have had to let him go. I guess you could say team-building camps in the nineties worked.

This team exercise coincided with the first months of marketing a new off-the-plan high-rise building in the city, which meant enormous pressure to achieve sky-high sales targets. A certain number of sales (about 50% of the total units) were required at that time for the developer to obtain finance. This was a tremendous challenge that had to be met for the development to proceed, and consequently, for all parties involved to get paid.

The key to realizing a dream is to focus not on success but on significance — and then even the small steps and little victories along your path will take on greater meaning.'

–Oprah Winfrey

Emotions ran high and everyone with a vested interest in the project was on tenterhooks until the stamp of approval from the financier came through. I was mentally exhausted and was dreaming of a stay at a 5-star Noosa resort, rather than the 'mozzie trap' teambuilding exercise I found myself on. All protocol went promptly out of the window when I completely lost it on the first day of trekking, screaming at one of the Special Forces guys at the top of my lungs, 'I hate you'.

But no one escaped these compulsory team bonding events, designed to create harmony amongst the sales agents and the rest of the team. But as sure as 'men and women can never be friends', so, too, 'real estate sales agents can never be team players'.

## Project marketing

A few months later, in another Monday morning sales meeting, one of the directors made an announcement: 'You're all fired'. Boom!

You could have heard a pin drop in the boardroom. My heart skipped a beat. I saw disbelief in the eyes of my colleagues, the facial expressions reflecting the bombshell just dropped on us. Then dumbfounded, we all stormed out of the boardroom and scrambled to come to terms with the change in events.

The focus of the business going forward was to be on project marketing, and our services were no longer required. Bad news indeed! The good news was it turned out to be the shortest sales meeting ever.

I was told that there was a project manager role coming up for an off-the-plan building of 120 units and I would be kept informed.

I was hoping for that to happen as soon as possible, but nothing happens fast in property development. Developers generally have a few projects on the go, to limit downtime whilst waiting for architects to draw up plans. Then comes the challenge of town planning approval and the toughest part of all, obtaining finance.

I had to keep the wolves from the door. I didn't have the luxury of waiting around for things to happen. Soon after leaving my first role, I started with a reputable boutique agency in the same area, the Western Suburbs.

Once established, it is not advisable to change offices. It's definitely not ideal, as it feels like starting from scratch each time, especially when moving into a new area. All the hard-earned knowledge and intricacies of the BDA will be lost. Even changing agencies within an area can mean a setback. Over the years I have seen agents hop in vain from one office to the next in pursuit of a different result.

Nevertheless, I enthusiastically submerged myself in the new office environment and continued my passion for selling real estate.

During this 'gap year', I loved bouncing into the office with my new sales agreements and the buzz of selling properties. I call it a 'gap year' in retrospect because it was only a year before the stars aligned and I started that project manager role with the high-rise tower in the Brisbane CBD.

# Chapter Six

# Positioning — Product

Which type of property are you attracted to? That's positioning. Positioning is also about your preference to either sell, lease, or manage residential or commercial properties. If you decide on residential real estate sales, will you specialise in apartments/townhouses or houses/land/development sites? Additional options are house and land packages or project marketing.

## Houses / Land / Units / Townhouses

When I started out, I sold residential real estate, both houses and units, in my BDA. This offered me the flexibility to obtain more listings. I couldn't afford to be picky, not until I had proven myself.

Truth be known, I never rejected any opportunity of a listing then, or at any time since in my career. This has been partly because I am terrible at saying NO, partly because it was good for consistent cash flow, and especially because I didn't like listings to end up with my competitors.

I loved the variety of real estate and I didn't mind working hard. (Have I mentioned that before?) Specialising in my specific BDA meant a perpetual cycle of meetings with clients already living in or interested in moving into my patch.

Subsequently, listing more properties resulted in more buyer inquiries and sales. For instance, if you market a property outside your BDA, once sold, all advertising benefits are lost. Whereas, focusing marketing efforts in a condensed area means the enquiries obtained from that marketing can be used for other properties indefinitely.

A simple equation to illustrate this: High number of listings in a specific BDA = High number of buyer inquiries = High number of sales

Some argue that it takes as much effort to sell a multi-million-dollar property as it takes to sell a cheap unit. But here is the thing: when markets turn down, cheaper properties keep selling. We have a saying in Germany, 'Kleinvieh macht auch mist', which literally means, 'Small animals s**t too' or 'Many pennies make a dollar'.

There were agents in our office who disliked handling the emotional aspects associated with house sales, and preferred the more clinical process of selling units. Others didn't like dealing with body corporates and the multitude of issues that come with selling in apartment blocks.

Units are often sold by interstate or overseas investors. This means all negotiations happen via phone or email. There are no lengthy around-the-table meetings discussing sales processes, buyers' feedback and 'why haven't we received offers two weeks into the marketing?'

"

# There is no magic to achievement. It's really about hard work, choices, and persistence.'

– Michelle Obama

The simple answer to that question is 'If the price is perceived as really good value in the marketplace, then often multiple offers are received early on. If not, then we have to work harder to find that premium buyer for you or reassess the price in a few weeks' time...'

Speaking from personal experience, agents prefer to just get on with the job, following up with interested parties and completing associated marketing for the property listing. Absent sellers let you do just that. Once they engage an agent, most times, that's it. They trust they are dealing with a professional who will achieve a sale with the best price possible in the prevailing market.

## Houses

There are houses and then there are beautiful homes, like I had in my first BDA, located in gorgeous tree-lined avenues in a prestigious area near a university, with first-class private schools, golf courses and upmarket shopping centres.

It was a real buzz when I could market and sell these attractive properties, though I learned over the years that, in general, the property I least expected to sell, sold first. This usually relates to price, and what is a popular product or a certain circumstance with purchasers at the time. It pays to actively find more of the kind of product buyers want, to increase your sales.

Incidentally, there are only four main factors that prevent a sale – price, presentation, poor marketing, and 'acts of the property god'. These include things like lengthy leases; a messy divorce where one party does not want to sell; unsatisfactory solicitor searches on things like easements; a seller changing their mind due to the property being rented to a family member; a property being re-zoned with a negative effect on the value; and the list goes on.

### Splitter blocks - when a house is not a house sale

A red-hot listing came my way! I had just signed up a house for sale on a splitter block. These mini-development sites are extremely popular with builders and small developers who split the land into two titles, then move the existing house to one side or remove it altogether. It is a worthwhile and profitable exercise.

Excited, I rushed back to the office and bounced in with my trophy listing. Splitter blocks generally meant an instantaneous sale.

What could go wrong? Lots, actually. There could be unknown easements; a large stormwater pipe running across the block; overland water flow issues; objections by neighbours; heritage listing on the house preventing it from being moved; not having access for two driveways because the frontage of the block was too narrow. Other than that, it was a straightforward sale. Ha-ha.

The existing house on this site was a post-war home, which was perfect as this property style is not listed on the Queensland Heritage Register. If it had been a style that is listed, such as a 'traditional Queenslander' home, that could have delayed the development approval and made the project more expensive due to required variations to the Development Application (DA). Variations are, for example, keeping certain features of the house, like a gable. This can make it more expensive for the buyer to renovate the property.

Additionally, if town planning requirements result in one or both of the new houses on splitter blocks becoming 3-bedroom instead of 4-bedroom residences, then the resale price goes down. It could also make the project unviable. In that case, the value of the property would drop dramatically, as it would need to be sold as a house, not a development site.

Most agents in our office were very well-connected to builders and developers. I was keen to protect my new listing and sell it myself, but I knew that as soon as it was written on the office for-sale board, all agents would launch into a phone frenzy and offers would come in thick and fast.

Multiple offers sound great but it can be tricky as there are inevitable losers, and this sale had to be dealt with carefully. My colleagues would try to quiz me on what the seller would accept, knowing fair well that, by law, I couldn't disclose this.

Every prospective buyer has to provide their best offer in regard to the price and conditions within the contract. There is only one chance to do so. Unfortunately, some buyers do not understand that notion and disputes arise. The listing agent presents all submissions to the seller for consideration.

It is illegal to reveal to any purchasers what other parties have submitted. Despite that, and not surprisingly, often the listing agent's buyer would miraculously come up with the best price or best conditions on their offer. Fortunately, so did my buyer! I sold this splitter block to one of the local builders who saw my for-sale sign outside the property.

In those days, I had just started to learn that some agents were holding back listings to get the first bite of the cherry. They then didn't have to share the commission with a 'conjuncting agent', which was generally as much as 40-50% of the fees.

But some of my colleagues also kept their new listings quiet and cleverly spread them out over a period to show a constant stream of new property listings in the Monday sales meetings.

## Units

Selling a unit versus a heritage-listed Queenslander is very different. A multitude of factors impact both property types, but the most prevalent for house sales is the emotional rollercoaster for sellers as they let go, being overprotective and believing the property is worth more.

I experienced these emotions myself when I sold one of my houses, so I totally understand. At first, I took buyers' comments far too personally until I put on my 'agent's hat' and rationally went through the sales process, to achieve top dollar for the street.

With unit sales, it's usually more an investment decision, and apartment sales are generally more clinical.

As I became more experienced, I knew property values in my BDA intimately. I was able to provide accurate market appraisals, and plenty of them, leading to a variety of listings with a consistent stream of sales, from beautiful Queenslander homes to hilltop units with city views.

Let's not forget the small six-pack units. These rect-angular buildings containing six residences were constructed in the 70s, mostly by Italian builders, and were renowned for being rock solid and practical but lacking in a certain style.

They were usually three-story walk-ups with no lifts, which meant low body corporate fees. Parents with university kids love them as investments. They sold relatively easily, and quickly became my bread-and-butter sales.

When listing an apartment, I like to get all the facts up front. If the property is not owner-occupied, I gather tenancy details, tenancy agreements, access and, possibly, the most recent entry condition report, furniture inventory, and the like.

Ideally, I like to invite the tenants for a coffee to introduce myself. Small gifts break the ice. The sales process must be as easy as possible for the tenants, since it impacts their home and lifestyle. I ask them for their preferences for inspections; whether they would like to stay on when their lease finishes; any maintenance issues; and, of course, I ask the question… 'Would you like to purchase the property?'

After renting a property for a while, tenants become emotionally invested and regularly offer top dollar to purchase their rentals.

On rare occasions, I could not win over the tenants, and they tried to move heaven and earth to prevent the sale. They'd use strategies such as leaving sharp objects on the lounge floor, or holding 'brunch parties' with their friends during open houses. The best strategy, in that case, is to not make a fuss but provide feedback to your seller. I would scale down inspections to an absolute minimum so the tenant couldn't refuse an inspection when a qualified buyer came along.

Qualifying a buyer means asking questions regarding their preferences for location, unit attributes, price (budget), finance, the timing of purchase in regard to the existing lease, and settlement preference.

After a while, when it came to the crunch with difficult tenants, the property manager and seller realized that the tenant was unreasonable. For me, it was a matter of 'give them enough rope and they'll hang themselves': I mean that in the nicest possible way.

It's a good idea to stay close to on-site managers of unit properties. I was in the fortunate position of specialising in sales only, and dealing with on-site staff was generally a breeze, as I always referred investors back to them for their services. I genuinely believe that's the best option for clients if the manager is a good operator. I would rather forfeit a referral fee with my other preferred contacts in order to act in the best interest of my clients.

However, depending on the ratio of owner-occupiers to investors in the marketplace, selling in unit blocks can cause friction when on-site managers lose business due to more people purchasing units to reside in, rather than rent out.

I rarely had issues but there were a couple of confronting incidences with irate managers. One emailed, about me, *'I have advised her in the past that I only want investors in here, and she underhandedly always finds owners.'* Then there was an official letter from a solicitor threatening legal action if I didn't *'immediately stop handing out chocolates to on-site staff'*. I was impressed!

Still, the reality was that employees did not like that sort of heavy-handedness from their superiors either, and continued to support me.

## Development sites/projects established and off the plan.

Sometimes changes in one's life simply happen because of others' decisions. I was presented with a fork in the road and chose off-the-plan property sales in 1999. From then on, a substantial part of my career entailed selling this type of real estate.

I managed two off-the-plan towers from start to finish and sold hundreds of apartments in various projects.

In the late 1990s, there was an upswing in the number of two-salary households, resulting in higher disposable incomes. At the same time, lending guidelines were relaxed and so was the tax system for property investors.

I was fortunate, as it was the perfect environment for investment sales and promoting off-the-plan projects. An apartment building boom followed in the early 2000s. This massive development wave carried me from project to project, right up to starting my own business in 2004.

So how is a high-rise building sold from scratch?

Developers generally engage in 'land banking sites': they buy land for future developments at today's prices, so they do not to miss out, or get caught short on, sites to develop. They then decide on the best usage for the land when planning the next project—that can be residential or commercial, or a mix of both.

Architects then design the building, maximizing the number of residential and commercial units within the project. Then the Council and appropriate authorities provide the DA, and the fun and marketing can begin. There are many costly hurdles before developers reach this point, and any delay means higher holding costs.

The project marketing team usually collaborates with multiple sales sources locally, interstate and overseas to promote the project. But ultimately, the on-site sales agent must have a stage presence and sell the dream. That was my job!

I inspected my brand-new workplace, the display suite right next to the vacant block of land where the building was to be. The showroom was complete with huge, impressive posters of panoramic views, a building model, promotional video, and boards showing finishing options, like colours, floor coverings, fittings etc.

Developers for larger buildings establish a whole display apartment to scale and replicate all aspects of the finished product. This makes it more realistic for purchasers and helps to create a feel for the apartment's layout and ambiance.

I settled into the show room quickly, imagined how the finished building would come alive, and visualised the views from the different apartments. I learned a script to present to interested parties, including other agents. Of course, it takes much more than that to succeed but that is where I began.

I studied all there was to know about the proposed project so I could answer any questions thrown at me. My confidence in the project had to shine through in all of my conversations. All buyers' doubts had to be put to rest for them to take the first step of placing a unit on hold. While I had a clinical structure for the presentations I gave, creating a strong relationship with my clients was paramount.

I became good at persuading people that they could not find a better product amongst the multiple proposed high-rise towers in town. And yes, I even convinced myself. That is what agents do—they start believing their own b*lls**t and buy their own properties. I was no exception.

## Selling and placing holds to unconditional

People visiting the display suite were pre-qualified. They were already sold on the location and price point. It was now up to me to ensure that interested parties were comfortable with the quality of the developer, builder, building manager and of course the product, including floor plans and finishes.

There are two simple questions I would ask: 'What is your budget?' and 'Are you an investor or owner occupier?' For this project, most were investors, but some wanted to reside there in the future. That enabled me to focus on which product was most suitable.

I developed a display suite sales routine. First, I welcomed the clients to ensure everyone felt comfortable. This included offering refreshments in the lounge and showing a promotional video as an introduction.

Afterwards, I clarified the different floor plans and choices for the interiors, utilising the building model and the finishes boards. All the while, soul music by Norah Jones played in the background.

When clients showed interest in a particular floor plan, we moved around the display, pacing out room sizes, checking materials, and envisioning the views of the prospective units. At that point, the buyers were invested and excited about the idea of owning one of the apartments.

Further discussion points were the existing and proposed infrastructures around the project, like the proposed building manager, the timeline of the construction, and which demographic was buying into the building.

Some purchasers would place a 'Hold' dot on the sales board and sign an Expression of Interest form so a contract could be prepared. Others arranged multiple inspections, checking in with their accountants and financial advisors, before making a buying decision.

I sold a lot of one-bed units with no car spaces to investors, which was a product not favoured by the banks although the rental returns were terrific, compared to two-bedroom units. Only buyers who could use equity in their residential homes were able to borrow money for this type of product, as deposit requirements were often as high as 30% to 40% of the purchase price.

I always recommended checking their investment options with their accountant or financial planner.

I learned over the years that when one door closes, another opens. Around the end of 2020, the popular option to purchase an investment property through superannuation funds came to a halt. This was because investors could not source funds for that type of investment. The banks didn't like to lend for this product and the government was concerned about the risk of not having enough investment diversification. Some investors wanted to use most of the super to purchase a property, which could have left them short of funds when going into retirement.

In 2022/23 sales data, it shows that one-bedroom units again became popular for investment, albeit not purchased through a super fund, as rent returns had skyrocketed. Young professionals who work in the CBD favour one-bedroom units as well, mainly for the convenience of city living, the price point, and of course the ability to sleep in on a work morning.

The other sought-after products are dual key apartments, particularly in well-managed serviced apartment buildings. A dual-key apartment is two separate, but adjoining units held under one legal title, accessed by one main entry into a small hall with two separate entry doors off that hall. The benefit for investors is double income. The owners have the option of using the apartment as a traditional owner-occupier unit to live in. Alternatively can choose to live in one part and rent out the other for additional income.

Incidentally, the attraction factor of a building rises and falls with the quality of the managers. Body corporate committees can keep tabs on maintenance and expenses, and influence the general upkeep of a building to a point, but inexperienced managers equal lower rental returns and capital gains for owners. I have seen firsthand how rental returns dropped from a healthy 9% gross to 5% gross when on-site managers changed and the quality of service declined.

The ultimate milestone for success for most off-the-plan projects appears in the early stages, when finance approval has been received and construction begins. Before that can happen, a certain number of unconditional contracts, usually 30% to 50% of the total number of units, need to be signed. Other strict lending criteria required buyers to submit a 10% deposit, and no changes to the sales contract were possible.

These unconditional contracts were then scrutinised by the banks' legal department and absolutely no disparities were accepted. Despite that, a few contracts were signed with changes but would not count for the bank's finance approval criteria.

Some buyers' solicitors would request the sunset clause to be shortened—the clause which fixes the maximum period within which an off-the-plan property must be completed. If the apartment is not finished by the maximum period (the sunset date) then the buyer can legally walk away and receive the full deposit back, except for the fees of a Bank Guarantee or Deposit Bond, usually a few thousand dollars.

Terminating the contract is fine for the buyer if the property market has not moved. On the other hand, if property values increased during the contract period, then there is a loss of opportunity. The buyer missed the chance to realise a potential profit for another property.

Sunset clauses usually include plenty of buffer years to cover any delays. On the flipside, it has happened that shorter sunset clauses in contracts allowed the developer to terminate contracts to resell the properties for more money.

An off-the-plan building needs to successfully settle in a timely fashion for everyone involved, including real estate agents, to be paid. Variations are another way that a project could run into financial trouble and slow down construction.

A variation can occur, for example, if the structural engineers missed including an extra pillar to hold up the building. A minor detail! The flow-on effect is disastrous, with valuable gross floor area (GFA) lost. The GFA is defined as the sum of the area of all floors of the building, measured from the external faces of the exterior walls. An additional column could result in fewer car spaces and/or smaller units, reducing the gross profit of the project.

In the later stages of high-rise construction, the key goal is to not run out of money due to building delays and variations, thereby reducing the developer's profit.

It's easy for a salesperson to be distracted or emotionally affected by this roller-coaster environment of moving targets—a shift in time frames for unconditional sales; various building issues and delays; changes to finance regulations for off-the-plan sales; and plenty of other hurdles. Speaking of which...

'EVERYONE OUT!' Dave, the foreman for the builder, shouted with urgency.

From my display suite, I had an excellent view over the adjoining construction site. One minute, I had watched at least six workers on small excavators digging and preparing the foundations alongside the wall of the neighbouring heritage government premises.

The next minute, I heard a massive thundering rumble that felt like an earthquake. I watched in horror as the entire heritage block next door crumbled into the building site. I was in shock. What happened to the construction staff and office workers in that building?

Thankfully, Dave had acted with lightning speed. Within minutes of small cracks appearing in the exterior walls in the next-door building, he had managed to warn all staff. He risked his life moving from floor to floor in the three-story heritage building to get everyone out. It was nothing short of a miracle. I still get goosebumps thinking about it.

The property development business is risky enough without delays due to whole buildings falling in. Shortly after the incident, Joe the developer walked into the sales suite. He kept a brave face and was philosophical. 'Hannah, I think now is a good time to tell each other the story of our lives,' and so we did, but neither can be printed here. He finished with, 'In 100 years, who is going to care?' It was his way of dealing with the situation. I still like using this phrase when things get tough.

Of course, any delays to the construction were a disaster and meant higher development costs and enormous danger that the project would to be unprofitable, to put it mildly. We were very aware of the potential impact, and we were not proven wrong. It took months to clear the site. Valuable documents and precious items had been stored in the Government building. The recovery was excruciatingly slow. Items were extracted by hand, as people scoured through the rubble methodically. The construction cost spun out of control. But the building did eventually settle.

## Sales cycle of off-the-plan projects

The sales cycle of promoting off-the-plan projects from launch to settlement involves three phases.

*Phase one* – the honeymoon period: This is the exciting first few months when everyone is in high spirits. An extensive advertising campaign is rolled out and the sales suite is buzzing; agents are enthusiastic, and buyers are keen to receive information and place 'Holds' on properties in the spirit of first-in-best-dressed.

*Phase two* – the endurance stage: This begins a few months into the marketing campaign. A routine of managing existing contracts and convincing new buyers that there is nothing wrong with the remaining apartments, which there generally isn't. Some units come back onto the market or the sales board for all sorts of reasons. One reason could be that a buyer can't organise finance or the 10% deposit. The preferred deposit option for off-the-plan purchasers is to provide a deposit bond or bank guarantee, as it is generally lower risk than to pay a cash deposit. Also, this money technically can be used to work for the buyer until settlement.

Notwithstanding this, I had one person rock up with a filled plastic bag of cash. Nervously, I said to the buyer, 'Okay, let's count the money.'

He said, 'Oh no, I am sure it will be fine.'

I went downtown to the bank and deposited the money, all the while with an uneasy feeling that I might get robbed. This happened around the year 2000. Nowadays, agents assist the government to combat money laundering by filing a Form 8300 if more than $10,000 in cash is received.

Some developers also like to withdraw certain apartments from sale and release them later. This of course enables the developer to time the market. That can backfire if the market goes down. In phase two, few buyers visit the sales suite and every lead needs to be followed up till the death. As construction progresses, updates provide opportunities to create more business.

*Phase three* – the end game: Few projects sell out in phase one or two. If they do, they are either keenly priced in a strong market, or the product is unique owner-occupier stock, well built by renowned developers, or in prime positions near parks or riverfront, universities, or similar.

Most projects have 10% to 20% of properties left for sale on building completion. In a challenging market (for example, in 2017) this percentage can be a lot higher.

Developers take huge risks and often get a bad rap in the community, but overall, they are visionaries who contribute enormously to our economy. This was particularly true when, by and large, the construction industry saved the Queensland economy after the mining downturn in 2016.

Buyers are generally oblivious to what goes on behind the scenes and are highly influenced by what they hear from the people they associate with: work colleagues, neighbours, friends, family, accountants, and financial advisors.

When a prospective purchaser walked into a display suite in 1999, they had heard from others that 'you will make money buying off the plan'. This was generally true for investors between 1999 and 2004, as they were purchasing in a rising market supported by high population increases, and it was almost foolproof. We were on the cusp of the property market moving up and the media, banks and financial advisors were relatively optimistic.

After about 2005, the market gradually changed: property prices increased for off-the-plan sales, but buyers were still sold on the idea that buying off the plan meant units would be worth more on settlement.

## Units off the plan 2017

Fast forward to 2017 and I was regularly approached to sell properties prior to them being settled. Once a nervous off-the-plan purchaser called me, as he was hoping to sell perhaps two of the four two-bed apartments he had signed for. I was speechless and thinking, *You did what? Buy four two-bed units off the plan in the same building for between $650 and $700,000?*

Who did this buyer trust to buy not one but four units, which in my view were overpriced by 20% to 30%?

Similarly established larger two-bed units with balconies (an absolute 'must have' in the Queensland climate), and with river or city views and better positioned, were selling for $500–$550,000 at the same time.

In 2017, some property valuers told me off the record that they automatically deduct at least $100,000 from the valuation of a new unit. Why? Because they believe this is what the prices were inflated by.

This meant that on the settlement of a new property, the purchasers could be faced with finding a substantial amount of extra funds. The alternative is to not settle and kiss the 10% deposit goodbye, and possibly be sued by the developer for the loss to on-sell the property.

I am not blaming the developer here as they are taking huge risks and need the funds to pay their creditors and/or make a profit for the shareholders.

A phenomenon I find difficult to understand is that a lot of buyers trust selling agents who share the same cultural backgrounds, regularly parting with large amounts of money to purchase multiple off-the-plan properties on their fellow countrymen's advice.

So, what is the secret to an off-the-plan purchase? Do your research and purchase from a reputable developer with a proven track record in buildings with a point of difference, ideally designed for owner-occupiers.

## Buyer's agent

Another career choice in real estate, which I have always been intrigued by, is to conduct business as a buyer's agent. It involves working with and acting solely in the best interest of the purchaser to secure their preferred property, from go-to-whoa.

It may be a good idea to check the prevailing property market before jumping in. It seems a sellers' market could make it a tough gig, because with limited stock available on the market, the search for the right property will take longer and dilute your income. I always liked the flexibility and idea of working as a buyer's agent. Maybe in my next life.

During my career in residential property, I have been fortunate to deal in most of the above sectors of the market, but was most aligned with, and possibly enjoyed … shhhh … selling units the most.

In a nutshell, 'positioning' is one of the most important factors to consider for real estate agents. Not just a buzzword, it forms the basis of creating a high-functioning, multifaceted network, leading to referrals and consequently a successful sales career. You choose!

"

# If it is to be, it is up to me.'

– William Johnsen

# KEY TWO

---

## Let your
## PASSION show

# Chapter Seven

# Charisma

When anyone selects a real estate agent to assist them with selling a property, they want to feel like they are choosing a good friend who is on their team. To work well with a client, the agent needs to be relatable— someone who provides professional and emotional support when issues arise, which is inevitable in sales.

How does your personality align with some of the successful agents in your area? Are you comfortable with being in a flexible work environment, where things change quickly from minute to minute? There are many personality types within real estate—the good, the bad and the ugly. Certain personalities suit some clients but not others.

Knowing your own personality type and primary traits can help you establish whether the work in a sales role in property would be a good fit for you.

## What characteristics are best suited to real estate sales?

There are over 2000 personality tests on the market, including the popular Myers-Briggs Type Indicator (MBTI®) and the DiSC® assessment.

The DiSC® model of behavior was first proposed in 1928 by William Moulton Marston, a physiological psychologist, in his book 'Emotions of Normal People'. And yes, it does apply to real estate agents.

Marston created the comic character, Wonder Woman, and strongly supported feminist ideas. One of his famous quotes was: 'Not even girls want to be girls so long as our feminine archetype lacks force, strength, and power'. Despite that, he also was also a polygamist! Go figure!

Here is a link to a fast online DiSC® assessment: after all, I do know from personal experience that salespeople have a very short attention span: www.discpersonalitytesting.com/free-disc-test/

The four DiSC® profiles are:

D – Dominance: moderately dominant, decisive and persistent, without being pushy; makes decisions; good problem solver

I – Influence: highly influential, people-oriented, enthusiastic, sociable and optimistic; will motivate and inspire

S – Steadiness: high stability, enables agents to gain trust and be patient with clients

C – Conscientiousness: place the emphasis on quality, accuracy, expertise, and competency.

Congratulations if you scored D in the DiSC® personality questionnaire. That profile is best suited to working as a property agent.

My test results showed a strong blend of D/I—dominance and influence—characterised as directive, quick-witted, results-oriented, self-reliant, and fast-paced. I excel at solving problems, and making things happen, and I am comfortable working with a diversity of people in varied environments.

Personality tests aside, the magic combination for an agent is to have a certain pizzazz and confidence that is noticed in the marketplace, which is then backed up with professional service. High energy and vitality are key. Without them, it's like dancing in the dark, waiting for something to happen. What is the fun in that? Turn on the lights and make clients feel fabulous in your presence.

In addition, knowing when to be decisive and when to be patient is a good skill in sales. Early in my career, other agents would often hand me the phone when they couldn't understand clients from other cultures whose English was limited, or who had a strong accent like me. My colleagues believed that, since English was not my first language, I would understand them perfectly. I didn't, but I was very patient and through careful listening I could get the gist of what they were trying to convey.

To be aware of your own personality type can help you adapt to the highly competitive and fast-paced nature of real estate, where people skills, flexibility and results are paramount. If you are not a 'D' personality type, worry not: a personal assistant may fill in your gaps and assist with, for example, organisational skills and attention to detail.

Perfectionism is in my DNA, perhaps with a little obsessive-compulsive behaviour thrown in, which I realise is not for everyone. Highly competitive, I was always fixated on winning that next listing, at the same time keeping all balls up in the air and providing a

150% level of service, with the aim of achieving best results for my clients.

I am sure a medical test would reveal the presence of a 'property gene', explaining my obsessive drive for all things property. I became a high-functioning happy property addict, getting a high out of helping people.

I had a one-track mind, fully focused on my monthly sales goals. I don't spend energy worrying about day-to-day setbacks, which are part of the game. Anyone can become a high achiever with the right mix of passion, hard work and complete attention to the desired sales goals.

In my business, the number of unit listings varied from twenty to thirty pieces of stock on offer at any given time. Still, I would always be on the hunt for more, to the point where once a young agent pleaded with me in a lobby of a high-rise building, 'Hannah, please leave some for us!'

My passion for selling properties resulted in a huge workload and a busy schedule with back-to-back appointments most days. It meant I was always running on high octane, literally, rushing in my turbocharged Saab convertible from one place to another in a timely fashion.

This sometimes got me into hot water with the authorities, like the time I rushed into the city from a meeting in the western suburbs. A Holden Commodore suddenly stopped in front of me at a set of lights just as they turned amber. I couldn't believe it, and promptly overtook the car to drive through the crossing on amber, or so I thought.

Sirens started blaring, and to my annoyance the vehicle turned out to be an undercover police car that then pursued me down the road. There was a lot of traffic, but eventually I decided to stop. One of the policemen approached me and asked why I was speeding. Adrenaline pumping, I said the first thing that popped into my head: 'I have to go to the ladies.' The policemen then discussed this amongst themselves and escorted me for one kilometer to the next public park with toilets. Let's just say I got off lightly.

Another time I had stopped at red lights on a major arterial road when I noticed a car next to me. The driver had a mustache and looked like something out of the Village People. He revved his engine, just a little. Hailing from Germany, that meant in no uncertain terms that he challenged me to a race. As the lights turned green, I took off and overtook him easily. You guessed it: again, sirens started screaming behind me. He turned out to be another undercover cop. It was 'Movember', and luck was on my side: he didn't stop. I laughed it off and carried on to my next appointment. It was another day in paradise.

Taking risks and getting caught is part of life (at least mine). It happens. It's exhilarating, a learning curve, and teaches resilience.

When I was due for a new car though, I bought a nice reliable family car to keep my demerit points in check.

## EQ

In Germany when you ask someone, 'How are you?', you would fully expect to listen intently for as long as it takes, whilst the other person tells you exactly what is happening in their life, warts and all. This was often true even in a professional setting. Healthy relationships start with understanding how the people you interact with feel.

Subscribing to this style of greeting helps to connect you with people from all walks of life and builds trust. It's important to take the time to listen to the happy stories as well as accounts of life's troubles, whether it's a client who just lost a property to another buyer or welcomed their first grandchild, or a reception staff member who is in distress over a boyfriend.

High emotional intelligence (otherwise known as emotional quotient or EQ) is, in a nutshell, the ability to understand, use and manage your own emotions in a positive way, and deal better with others. EQ is linked to better communication, problem-solving, and increased social skills, leading to professional success.

While working on another off-the-plan project, I had been marketing a city apartment tower for seven months and was ready to move on to another challenge. To alleviate boredom, I was already completing a Diploma in Financial Advising and had freshened up on my Italian language skills.

It was yet again a quiet Sunday in the display suite. I was starting to get concerned, with Monday morning's sales meeting approaching fast. Thirty percent of units were left to sell in this project and everyone, especially me, was keen to wrap it up sooner than later.

In an industry notorious for high staff turnover, I was bucking the trend and wanted to persevere to complete sell out. Why? Because it aligns with my value of doing the right thing.

Fortunately, in real estate changes happen quickly. Just when I was about to lock up for the day, a man in sneakers and a cowboy hat walked through the door. To say I was very happy to see him was an understatement. I ignored his attire and took my time explaining every aspect of the project to him. It was an enjoyable experience and we had fun.

I was blown away when he spontaneously placed three units on hold. Still recovering from my surprise, he added he would refer some of his associates to me, which a few weeks later resulted in five additional sales.

During my career I had extraordinary sales events like this happen a few times a year and they certainly were very much appreciated—and made up for the 80% of more problematic sales. Call me naïve or an optimist, but I always expect the best from people.

It's worth knowing your EQ score, as emotional intelligence translates to good customer relationships. There are plenty of free EQ assessments available online, to provide you with insight. Some, which are endorsed by Harvard Professional Development, are found at Psychology Today, Mind Tools and the Institute for Health and Human Potential.

Real estate is a passionate business. Managing the pace starts with controlling your emotions by appreciating how you tick. You need to learn how to adapt to different situations with ease and focus on results, instead of wallowing in setbacks.

Show empathy, put yourself in people's shoes, and be aware of what needs to be done to get a good outcome. Establish trust and gently guide and inspire clients to a mutually beneficial conclusion.

Improve your emotional intelligence by getting to know and heal yourself first, so you can grow and foster better relationships and attract success for those in your influence.

## First-class listener

Are you worried about not having the right personality traits for success? Don't be: just be a first-class listener!

The ability to actively and respectfully listen when in conversation with clients, so you can fully understand their requirements and action them, is a must-have skill for a property agent.

Julian Treasure, the CEO of Sound Agency, explains: 'We spend roughly 60% of our communication time listening, but we are not very good at it and we retain just 25% of what we hear'.

Julian has five tips on how to pay attention to your clients and access understanding:

1. Practise silence for three minutes a day.
2. Sit quietly in a café or in nature and count the different sounds you can hear.
3. Savour mundane sounds: These are like hidden choirs around us all the time – e.g., a tumble dryer may sound like a waltz.

4. Be aware of your listening positions: We give unconscious attention to a whole range of filters, such as the filters of 'culture' or 'gender'. We can choose what is appropriate, and become either critical or empathetic during conversations.

5. Remember the acronym 'RASA', which means 'juice' or 'essence' in Sanskrit: it stands for 'Receive information; Appreciate the other's viewpoint; Summarise what the client conveyed; Ask questions to reinforce the client's goal'.

I constantly remind myself to make all my meetings with clients count. Listening and establishing a relationship always comes first.

Don't tell your clients your troubles: they are not interested. They don't care that your car broke down; that you had a dentist appointment; or that some other health issue is on your mind. It's not about you. In fact, certain cultures believe that if someone's life is chaotic, that's bad feng shui, and clients may not like to buy property from you.

Lou Holtz went a step further…

'Never tell your problems to anyone: 20% don't care and the other 80% are glad you have them.'

After greeting your clients, zip it. Listen and let the world revolve around them. When you ask questions, address everyone by their name. Be enthusiastic, open, and approachable:

'Jane, did you find the visitor car park easily?'

'Jane, have you inspected any other properties today? And did anything jump out at you?'

'What did you like or dislike, Jane – and what would your ideal property look like?'

Not only will you learn a lot about the individual's requirements, but research shows that using someone's name in conversation is polite and respectful, and it also makes clients feel valued.

In today's fast-moving world – especially at the open house frenzies on Saturdays – it's a good tool to grab buyers' attention and make the experience more memorable.

Effective listening demands that a person is fully present and intuitively interprets what is being said in both words and body language.

One time in my career, I was going into battle to list a very sought-after development site in an inner-city suburb. It was a deceased estate with four brothers as beneficiaries. I had arranged to meet with two of them at the property to be sold.

More than two owners on a title deed happens to be every agent's worst nightmare. This time there would invariably be four different opinions and four parties to convince to list... and later four people to agree to sign the contract.

As the house had already been cleared of furniture, I was offered a box that doubled as a makeshift chair in the empty lounge. I was fully prepared to spend several hours with them and learn everyone's motivation. The two brothers had brought their wives, so sitting on my box, I had four people eyeballing me now, giving me their full attention. I politely offered my condolences and asked if they'd grown up in this house.

Then Mike, the oldest brother, and Simon his younger sibling, took turns in filling me in on the family history and the property attributes.

They told me their mum, Betty, had loved to sit in the sunroom overlooking the garden. I learned how long she had lived in the house, and how the neighbours had helped her out, and that she baked the best scones. I shared that my mum in Germany liked baking a cake every day, and sympathised that those times were very precious.

They told me that the shed in the backyard still needed to be cleared of the items that were stored there. Then I heard about the location of the stormwater pipes, the dimensions of the block, and the asbestos roof.

I paraphrased some of the facts they told me. The conversation flowed smoothly, and I calmly answered all the questions both brothers and their wives fired at me.

'Do you think you can achieve the price range you have provided in the market appraisal?'

'What other similar sites have you sold recently in the area?'

'Who are your contacts? Have you got buyers?'

'Why do you think you are the best company for the sale?'

A few hours later, the brothers told me that they felt comfortable giving me the job and Brian, one of the other siblings, would trust their judgment.

Mike explained that Dave, the youngest brother, may not be so easy to deal with. Apparently, he was always the odd one out. Dave was keen to sell the property through one of his friends, a specialist agent for development sites. Unsurprisingly, I was already aware that other agents were in the mix. I had spoken with one of my own builder clients prior to the meeting, and he told me he had been approached by another agent regarding a property with uncannily similar attributes in the same area.

I smiled and said, 'That's fine, Mike, I understand his concerns. Please ask Dave to phone me to discuss the sale.'

A few days later, I received the call, and as Mike and the other brothers had laid the groundwork with Dave, we finished the conversation with him reluctantly agreeing to list with me.

During the sales process, the other rival agent checked in with Dave on a weekly basis to tell him he had buyers with high-price offers—it's an illegal practice but is not monitored, so its illegality is on paper only. Hostile phone calls from Dave ensued, but luckily the other brothers believed in me and defended my work. The pressure was on to achieve a good price quickly, within the sales agreement period.

Finally, after presenting a few offers from different parties, I met with the same builder who was approached by the other agent in the beginning. Sometimes sellers agree verbally to an offer but when meeting up they have changed their mind. Argggh. Not this time! After an afternoon round trip to all four parties, I managed to have the contract signed. And the builder paid a premium price. Just like in the song 'Sweet Victory', performed by David Glen Eisley, 'the winner takes all'.

Apart from my competitive nature, it's clear that the value of listening and excellent people skills can't be overlooked. Once again, the soft touch led the way to success.

# Chapter Eight

# All Things Ethics

A healthy set of ethics is the most important attribute for an agent… or anyone who desires to be successful. It entails a lot of hard work, going the extra mile, and diligently completing all tasks on the daily to-do list, even when additional appointments have cropped up.

## Strong work ethics

Clients recognise strong work ethics and reward these agents with business and referrals. Hardworking agents experience a perpetual cycle of sales. Each new listing and sale is significant, and will ideally lead to more business. This is a simple sales growth strategy—provide 150% service each time.

Why doesn't everyone have a positive set of work ethics? Research shows it comes back to an individual's values, sense of self, and grit.

Growing up in Germany in the 70s, I had strong role models. My grandmother Emma brought up five children on her own during World War II, as did her sister, my Auntie Katharina! Single, strong as an ox (I mean that in the nicest possible way), with self-confidence to match, Grandmother Emma could make any grown man cry. For these resilient women, working hard meant survival, whilst for us, they instilled a positive attitude to work.

Some religions advocate hard work too. The Protestant work ethic emphasises the importance of discipline and diligence in your profession. As a good Catholic girl, I was exposed early on to the theological concept of care and hard work, and laziness was frowned upon. My mum would constantly quote German proverbs to influence our behaviour, like 'Des Teufels liebstes Moebelstueck ist die lange Bank', meaning 'Putting something on the long bench that you could take care of right now means the devil wins'.

When I started my real estate career I would now and then—okay, make that regularly—question my abilities when sales were slow, and I'd confide in one of my Italian friends, Gina. She would say to me: 'But Hannah, we're emigrants; we just work harder. We're workers; we just make it happen.'

True, when I left the 'Fatherland' I made uncertainty my friend and adapted to new challenges fast. I developed an 'immigrant mindset': failure was not an option!

One's sense of self—how you think about your own abilities—is reflected in either positive or negative self-talk. It can be slightly exaggerated, like 'I don't care how good you are, I am better' or 'I am not good enough; I can't do it'.[1]

Get to know how you tick, beware of your internal dialogue, and if necessary, correct it with self-development. Negativity puts the brakes on productivity and leads to mediocre outcomes.

Practice makes perfect. Perform affirmations as DIY motivational pep talks to stay focused on your goals. Be kind and sympathetic with yourself: 'I am strong, and I will become the top sales agent.' 'I am awesome: I can handle it.' '"No" means I am one step closer to my next listing.'

Unlike self-control, which is all about forming good habits for positive outcomes, willpower helps us resist short-term temptations to achieve long-term goals. The key to success is being a self-starter who is self-disciplined and productive... but that can be easily jeopardized by daily stressful situations.

Beneficial lifestyle habits that support your brain to make good decisions are vital. Strong willpower feeds on getting enough quality sleep, physical exercise, daily meditation, eating well, and absolute focus on your plan.

Additionally, research suggests that doing good for others improves willpower. Kurt Gray, a researcher at Harvard University, found that when people donated money to charity or thought about helping another person, they were able to hold up weights for a longer time than those who didn't engage in pro-social thoughts or actions. According to Gray, helping others heightens willpower and self-control. As he suggests: 'Perhaps the best way to resist the donuts at work is to donate your change in the morning to a worthy cause.'

By doing good and by cultivating positive emotions, we inoculate ourselves against temptation and immediate gratification.

Bad habits don't have to stay with you forever. Continuous self-development will lead to a life of achievement, strengthening your standards and your sense of self-worth and determination, and nothing will be impossible.

## Integrity

Integrity is doing the right thing (through your words, actions and beliefs) when no one is watching. It means taking responsibility for one's actions, being trustworthy, and basing decisions on your principles rather than personal gain.

Adherence to moral principles is one of the most important traits for an agent, yet it is lost on many. Some defend their bad behaviour by saying, 'That's business'.

Sometimes lines are crossed unintentionally but ignorance is no excuse.

It was early on in my career, and I had just listed a small two-bed unit in a six-pack building. It was in an excellent position close to shops in an attractive tree-lined street, and whilst not in the best condition, it had an attractive price point.

**"**

**There is no royal, flower-strewn path to success. And if there is, I have not found it. For if I have accomplished anything in life, it is because I have been willing to work hard.'**

– CJ Walker, Madame CJ Walker
Manufacturing Company

Viewing the property through my rose-colored glasses, I ignored various negative aspects. These became clear as soon as my colleagues inspected the property on the Monday morning caravan. The unit needed work; the building aesthetics were neglected; the garden needed attention. The list of problems went on and on. It became obvious the list price was too high.

After a couple of months of hosting open house sessions, and a price adjustment, I finally had a first home buyer, Jordan, who was interested. He made an offer that was accepted by the seller after I had provided plenty of honest feedback from the market.

The offer was subject to finance, and a building and pest inspection. At the buyer's request, I had recommended a few building inspectors who were called on regularly in our office to assist clients.

The building inspection report came back fine, with only a small number of items needing attention, but nothing too drastic.

The long and the short of it was that a few months after settlement the buyer called me to let me know that the building had structural issues. I was shocked and felt immediately responsible because I had given him the names of the building inspectors.

The saving grace was that the unit block itself was in such a sought-after street on a large size parcel of land that the land itself had appreciated enough for the buyer to make a capital gain when the unit block was sold for development a few years later.

I learned my lesson! After that incident, when a buyer asked for advice, I stayed neutral. If a client asked, 'Hannah, do you think I need a building inspection on this unit?' I would reply, 'That is entirely up to you.' If they asked, 'Do you or your family have a contact for a building inspector?' I rarely provided contacts to buyers.

As a side note, the land size of a unit building is rarely considered by property investors, but it could be the thing to capitalise on when the land becomes more valuable than the building. Owner occupiers can get caught out if they renovate their apartment shortly before other residents wish to sell to a developer. This sort of thing regularly causes friction within a building's community.

So remember, if you are interacting with the buyer, be cautious with recommendations. There can be pitfalls.

Firstly, as real estate agents, we work for the seller and aim to achieve the best result possible. Affiliate companies work for real estate offices, toeing the line for continued business with that company.

It shouldn't happen, but I have witnessed building inspectors providing soft reports, and mortgage brokers pushing finance deals to stay in the good books with agents. Once again, don't cross that line to the dark side.

## Honesty

Another key trait of a high-producing agent is honesty. That's not always easy for some—'what's the harm in a little white lie?'—but lies will come back to haunt you and your reputation. Conveying the facts to clients with polite and open conversations earns trust and respect, and is *always* the right thing to do.

Time and again, property sellers have made me feel privileged when they tell me 'everything', and trust me not to use it against them. They may disclose medical issues, or that they have bought another property and the pressure is on to sell, or even what price they would accept. This is exactly how it should be between client and agent, when you have established good customer relationships and are recognised as an ethical businessperson.

Early in my career, I remember receiving a phone call from a lovely older gentleman, Robert, and his wife Dorothy, a couple who had been living in their very sought-after home in the western suburbs of Brisbane for their entire married life.

The property happened to be sitting on a unit development block, which in those days was like gold. I was nervous before meeting them, as the competition was fierce with plenty of experienced agents fighting over the listing. I knew, if I listed this trophy property, it would result in a quick sale.

I shouldn't have worried; we clicked straight away. They were delightful, showing me through their family home with ease, and we went down memory lane together. I listened patiently to all the family stories, sadness creeping into their voices, as they were acutely aware they must leave it all behind.

I felt for them and promised to make the sale as painless as possible. Before I left the meeting, Robert took me aside and whispered, 'We don't want to sell the house to the neighbour. We don't like or trust him – he just wants to pull down the house and build units.'

There was no reasoning with Robert; I explained to no avail that often neighbours pay a higher price as they already love the street and the position, and a developer generally pays more than a traditional house buyer.

Then I started the marketing campaign and got a reality check quick smart, as I listened to potential buyers' feedback. 'Great views but the land is too steep for our children to play in.' 'Putting in a pool is too expensive.' 'There is too much work to be done on the wooden structure of the house.' 'The street frontage is not wide enough.' 'The property is too close to the units next door.' 'It's risky as the house might not be able to be removed'. And so the property sat on the market unsold for months.

Out of the blue, George, the next-door neighbour, called me. He told me that an overseas client would be investing in multiple properties, and he wanted him to purchase the house.

What to do? Technically, the neighbour wouldn't be buying the property! Then why did I have a knot in my stomach and a bad feeling about this?

In the ensuing weeks, George kept me abreast of the progress. Alexander couldn't bring his money into the country yet, as he was getting divorced and had to be careful, otherwise his ex-wife could 'grab the monies'.

Finally, George told me that Alexander was now in Sydney, and he would arrive in Brisbane the following week. They intended to inspect and buy properties together.

Then Alexander's money was still delayed, and George paid the deposits for signed contracts on various properties.

I was invited to have lunch with George and his client at a posh restaurant, a popular meeting place for business lunches, and George paid the bill.

Alexander was of impressive stature, confident and charismatic. You would not question that he was the real deal. George arranged for Alexander to test drive a Ferrari that afternoon, after lunch. Life was becoming surreal, but we were all on a high and I didn't think twice about it. After all, it was the late 90s and the economy was on an upswing!

Eventually, I received the entity (name) for Alexander's purchase and prepared the contract for Robert and Dorothy's property. It was for the full asking price, so why would I question it?

I met with Alexander in his serviced apartment to sign the contract. As soon as I entered, the hairs stood up on the back of my neck: that bad feeling returned. To my surprise, George's wife was in the unit too, looking slightly dishevelled as she emerged from the bedroom to greet me.

Ignoring that fact—none of my business—and keeping my eyes firmly on the ball, he enthusiastically signed the contract.

After that meeting, it took forever for the deposit to be paid. Unexpectedly, George called me a few weeks later to terminate the contract using a special condition. George begrudgingly explained that Alexander was a conman and had made a 'run for it'. I was stunned; all of Alexander's compelling, farfetched stories had tricked us all.

Robert and Dorothy were suspicious of the legitimacy of the buyer from day one and were not in the least surprised that the contract fell over. They were pleased when a local couple with two children bought the house, and their legacy could live on.

I learned a couple of lessons: there are no shades of honesty—either it is, or it is not. And I learned the importance of listening to your gut instincts. If it sounds too good to be true, it probably is.

# Chapter Nine

# Persistence

Persistence is the most important personality trait for a successful real estate agent—a dogged determination to make sales with a 'never give up' attitude. Setting goals is easy; the tough part is to fight for them until the sweet end.

## Resilience

Everyone works differently: some are more productive in the morning while others are night owls. The key is to develop strategies that work for you, and the know-how to break through the pain barrier when things get tough.

Truly realise how valuable every minute of the day is, and stay one step ahead of the schedule, whether that means staying up all night to finish a listing presentation or a mailout to the database, or missing a weekend event with friends to show an interstate buyer around properties.

Relentless rivalry is an ever-present visible and nonvisible undercurrent in real estate. However, my biggest foes in business were not my competitors, but... wait for it... media sources. Extreme news reports, which varied from good to mostly bad to downright 'fake news', always grab attention, and that made my life in business feel like I was riding a tumultuous roller coaster.

It's extremely challenging to stay passionate through the constant white noise of the media cycles, which can cause property markets to slow for no apparent reason.

Most of the relevant reporting in Australia originates from media in the southern states talking about southern property markets. Every negative report still affects the Queensland property market, regardless of the fact that property markets are very different from state to state, in regard to capital gains, rent returns, prices fluctuations, and over- and under-supply in the market.

"

When the world says,
"Give up", Hope
whispers, "Try it one
more time".

– Anonymous

Property news is at the forefront of buyers' and sellers' minds and discussed at length around the barbeque. An agent needs to be prepared with appropriate research for any tricky questions like: 'Hannah, I hear the market is going down?' My answer would be: 'Sure, if you are buying in X city where the market has already moved by X%, you would be a little concerned. The reality is, I don't believe you could build this particular property again for the same price in the current market. Add to that the upcoming X billion in infrastructure and we're talking about a completely different market scenario.'

I was always able to support my comments with credible, solid statistics for upcoming infrastructure spends, sales and rental information, and graphs for leading indicators for Queensland's economy regarding resource investments, tourism, and population growth.

On that note, don't believe everything you read in the news, but who has the time to research? Well, the agent must. For example, I once read an article where a certain building (and for that matter, the whole suburb) was reported as the place for unit investment, as it showed the highest capital returns in the preceding year. When I dug a bit deeper, I noticed that 'one entity with generous access to funds' paid top dollar for multiple units within the complex, which had pushed up the capital gains.

Real estate agents do get dragged down by the negative news and then start whining: 'Oh the market is terrible', 'There are no buyers', 'Interest rates are going up', 'Property prices are going down'. Negativity takes over and that's all they can focus on, instead of doing the basic ABCs of real estate—like following up leads, making calls to the database, meeting up with clients, and 'shaking that tree to see what falls out'. It becomes a vicious cycle.

Personally, I was fortunate that, working as a boutique business, I didn't have that negative talk around me. Sure, when sales went down for a month, and then even further the next, I would question, 'Is it me?' I always learned later that the larger agencies were experiencing the same.

The bottom line is, consistency and persistence get a property agent through the roller coaster of negative media and market downturns.

Property markets can change up or down quickly. Over the years, I would get concerned when the phone stopped ringing or absolutely no internet inquiries came in, to the point where I would check with my long-suffering IT people whether there was a fault in my system.

66

# What you focus on is all that you will see.'

– Justin Herald

Incidentally, excellent (and costly) IT support was non-negotiable for me as any disruptions could affect business dearly. If problems occurred, it turned me into a caged lioness till the system was up and running again. Those poor IT people I dealt with must have kept training companies busy with their need for development courses on 'How to deal with difficult customers'!

A grassroots issue, and a trap agents fall into, is forgetting to steadily list properties. It's easy to get caught up in servicing listings and enjoying a good sales run … and then nothing!

Giving attention to chasing up new business must be an equal priority, if not more so, than attention to sales activities. It's vital to consistently conduct listing activities to keep new stock rolling in. Over the years, I found focusing my energy on prospective sellers more valuable than chasing up buyers. As a rule, interested purchasers will be in touch.

It might sound weird to you, but most times I would know straight up when I met with a buyer whether or not they would be 'the one'. Almost like déjà vu, their voice would sound familiar and there would be some commonality with the seller. For example, the buyer and seller might have both been ex-pats from the same location or similar circumstances; or both parties might have had the same profession. It's an unexplained phenomenon to me: some may be skeptical and call it a coincidence, but I put it down to heightened intuition.

On occasion, 'pseudo buyers' from rival companies made an appointment with me. I could smell them a mile away. They were trying to snatch the property details (to get in touch with the seller) and sometimes even trying to find out the secrets to how I ran my business.

I think they were always disappointed that there was no magic bullet. My 'secret' was simply working hard, listing a huge number of units, and consequently registering more buyers on my database, which lead to more business. Add a massive dose of resilience to the equation. That's it!

People are always surprised when I tell them that the market has been tough in Queensland for a long time, dealing with the global financial crisis in 2007, floods in 2011, an oversupply of apartments peaking in 2018, combined with a tightening in finance and restrictions on foreign investors taking money out of their country of origin.

What do you do when one in three deals falls over because of finance? How do you deal with the many setbacks in real estate?

Harvard Business Research ran a story with Martin
E.P. Seligman, 'the father of positive psychology', on
building resilience. 'We discovered that people who
don't give up have a habit of interpreting setbacks
as temporary, local, and changeable. ("It's going
away quickly; it's just this one situation, and I can do
something about it.") That suggested how we might
immunize people against learned helplessness, against
depression and anxiety, and against giving up after
failure: by teaching them to think like optimists.'

Seligman explains: 'In November 2008, when the
legendary General George W. Casey, Jr., the army chief
of staff and former commander of the multinational
force in Iraq, asked me what positive psychology had
to say about soldiers' problems, I offered a simple
answer: How human beings react to extreme adversity
is normally distributed.

'On one end are the people who fall apart into PTSD,
depression, and even suicide. In the middle are most
people, who at first react with symptoms of depression
and anxiety but within a month or so are, by physical
and psychological measures, back where they were
before the trauma. That is resilience. On the other
end are people who show post-traumatic growth. They,
too, first experience depression and anxiety, often
exhibiting full-blown PTSD, but within a year they are
better off than they were before the trauma. These are

the people of whom Friedrich Nietzsche said, "That which does not kill us makes us stronger.""[2]

I once negotiated a deal for a 2-bed unit with Sakura, a lovely Japanese lady. It was her first purchase in Australia, and she was nervous and in need of guidance. I straight away had a soft spot for her.

As agents, we facilitate sales and manage all parties involved. By law, we are not allowed to provide financial or legal advice, but sometimes even solicitors need a little assistance.

Sakura purchased a property, and the contract became unconditional. Unbeknown to me, she instructed her solicitor a week out from settlement to bring it forward by a few days to a Friday, the 21st. Unfortunately, the buyer's solicitor was sitting on this request and only actioned it two days before the buyer's expected settlement. Consequently, all hell broke loose.

The seller did not agree to the earlier date, as he was still organising additional funds for settlement to cover his mortgages. I suggested to the seller to request having part of the buyer's deposit released earlier to keep the bank happy.

The deposit is generally held in the Real Estate Agents Trust account and forms part of the settlement, in this case, the extra amount needed to pay out the seller's mortgages.

Sakura kept calling me, insisting that settlement must happen on Friday the 21st. She then revealed that she could not settle the property after that date, even if she lost her deposit, as it would fall into an unlucky period. Her stars turned negative from the 22nd onwards and it would be bad luck to settle the property for another 45 days.

I conveyed this unusual situation to the seller and, this time, he instructed his solicitor to request an early release of the part deposit and include a clause in the contract to protect the buyer's deposit monies, just in case settlement did not take place on the Friday because the banks were not ready, or any other problems occurred. This was important as it prevented the buyer from losing their part deposit once it was handed to the seller.

The afternoon of Friday the 21st arrived, and adding to the drama, the seller's conveyancer had gone home sick, around lunchtime.

After navigating around the 'rottweiler receptionist', I finally spoke with the director of the seller's solicitor firm. Thankfully he was on the ball and sprang into action.

Then the seller's bank had a technical issue across all of their departments late in the afternoon and the solicitors had trouble getting through to the settlement line.

Finally—and amazingly—the property settled on Friday the 21st. The force of the Property God was with me!

There is often no rhyme or reason to why some properties sell early, and some take longer. I remember conducting 10-plus open houses and numerous inspections on a unit in a busy high-rise building. The 90-day exclusive listing with an interstate seller was just about to expire.

Another agent had been pestering my client for weeks—an illegal practice some unethical agents engage in. This agent promised an easy sale, a higher price and, of course, the oldest trick in the book… 'We have a buyer waiting for your property'.

The seller, whilst sympathising with me, was understandably rattled. He wished to list his property with the other agent, after all he was promised an easy sale. Not giving in, I asked my seller to allow me to conduct one last open house. As we did have a good relationship and I had kept him informed during the selling process, I was able to convince him.

# Perseverance is the hard work you do after you get tired of doing the hard work you already did.'

– Newt Gingrich

As luck would have it, I showed an investor from Sydney through the property. He had already inspected one of my other apartments and I persuaded him to check out this one, too. Unbelievably, he made a successful offer that day. I was thrilled!

I have lost many listings to other agents over the years, and it always dismayed me when the consequent sale ended up being way below the list price I had for the property.

## Passion

In Europe, people live in their property almost all of their life, so talking about real estate is not really on anyone's conversation agenda—a complete contrast to Australia, where everyone is obsessed with property. As soon as I disclosed I was a real estate agent, the conversation floodgates opened with good and bad real estate stories, and questions about the market.

Passion is a prerequisite for life as a property agent—a love for all things real estate, and especially dealing with people. An agent must not make their career all about earning a commission; they have to genuinely care about helping change peoples' lives. Being enthusiastic and making real estate a lifestyle choice will ultimately reap the rewards over time. But that doesn't mean it will be an easy profession. After all, the Latin verb for passion, 'patere', means to suffer.

Then there is another kind of passion. I had arranged an inspection for a serviced apartment unit choosing a slot in between guests checking out and new ones coming in. As I always do, I knocked forcefully on the door a few times. As expected, there was no answer, and my buyer, Sean, and I strode into the property.

Once seen, some things can never be unseen, and this was one of them. Two male occupants looked at us in surprise whilst... how can I label it... entangled in a compromising position.

Sean fell backward in shock. Not missing a beat, I said, 'Oh sorry – can we come back in five minutes?' To my surprise, they agreed, though Sean refused categorically to enter the unit again that day, so we rescheduled. Despite his shock, Sean did buy the unit.

\*     \*     \*

Another drama in a busy Saturday open unit session in a high-rise. A loud bang and flickering lights in the elevator, then complete silence. The lift stopped and I was squashed together with six buyers plus another real estate agent in an apartment tower in the Brisbane CBD.

Bugger! I am afraid of tight spaces and panicked, but of course, I didn't want to alarm my clients. I felt responsible for them. I took a deep breath and sprang into action by pressing the emergency call button. A nice voice answered and wanted me to spell my name. I obliged, 'S C H U H...', then everyone started shouting, 'JUST GET US OUT!' The operator assured us that help was coming.

After 30 minutes, I started to worry that the air was getting thin. It got hot quickly, and I was running out of jokes. 'I will take off my jacket, but that's the only thing I take off!' and 'Is now a good time to talk about the benefits of this building?'

Then the other agent collapsed onto the floor, and a large burly man from Melbourne joined her. With the help of a client, I pushed a shoe through the lift doors to let in air. At the same, I was telling the other agent to *breathe in 1, 2, 3 and out 1, 2, 3.* It was surreal – me, helping another agent to live?

The drama ended almost two hours later, when firemen with axes broke open the lift doors just wide enough to rescue us.

Reporters were waiting outside and wanted comments. No time for that; my adrenalin was still pumping, and I persuaded one of the interstate couples from the lift to come to another apartment block to show them a unit. Another successful sale after a tough day.

You may encounter many defeats,
but you must not be defeated.
In fact, it may be necessary
to encounter the defeats, so
you can know who you are,
what you can rise from, how
you can still come out of it.'

– Maya Angelou

## Attention to detail

Another trait agents benefit from is high attention to detail, important to both property presentation and contract administration.

This is in my DNA, or maybe it's just because I suffer from a touch of OCD, aka Obsessive Compulsive Disorder. I take great pleasure in presenting properties just perfectly prior to inspections or open houses ... a final polish of a coffee table, rearranging flowers, or a final check for anything out of place.

Once, I was about to start the first open house for a luxury riverfront apartment. I was super proud of having listed this awesome property and I wanted everything to be just right—professional marketing material, flowers, chocolates, lights on, windows and doors open, 'remove your shoes' sign on the doorstop in the entry door.

Arrgh! My eye caught the tiniest piece of paper lying outside on the carpet in the lift corridor.

One shoe still in hand, I quickly picked up the tiny fleck so the place was presented perfectly. Whooshka! The river breeze shut the entry door behind me, leaving me on the wrong side without a key. OMG. My bag and phone were inside. I had to let the queue of keen buyers know that the open house would be rescheduled for later that afternoon, after the locksmith had a chance to unlock the door. The devil was literally in the detail.

Attention to detail is crucial when scheduling all deadlines for contracts and when drawing them up in the first place. If you miss something, or have the wrong details, it could cause the contract to crash later. Take the time to peruse documents a few times: better still, print them out and make sure they are 100% right. Your reputation depends on it.

There are plenty of stories of where agents have let clients down badly. I once had a buyer tell me that another agent didn't show up to scheduled inspections three times in a row. This agent used a dental appointment as a defence each time. He either had very bad teeth or was very unprofessional.

Agents need to be disciplined and consistently follow through on commitments: be punctual for appointments, deliver more than promised, delight your clients by going the extra mile, and above all, be prepared. That is key.

## Work/life balance

There is no work/life balance for a real estate agent. If you want to be successful, property is your life! I agree to disagree with anyone who says otherwise.

I have been to plenty of seminars where gurus have tried to convert me and tell me that it's possible to have a work/life balance. Strategies to achieve this included making all your phone calls in blocks at certain times of the day, and applying the same to responding to emails. To that, I say politely in my best English, 'Bollocks'.

To provide the best service—better than your competition, who are top-producing real estate agents—you must respond straight away every time! And I don't mean just sending a text either! Current clients especially need to hear your voice often: they want to feel supported and know that you're working hard for them.

When a seller calls to list their property and there is no answer, they will go elsewhere: there are plenty of other agents who will pick up the phone. Liz, an agent I once worked with, learned that the hard way. She had driven up to Mount Tamborine in the Gold Coast hinterland south of Brisbane, an area with limited mobile phone reception, when a seller tried to phone her. She only received the message a few hours later, and when she called back, this seller had listed the property with another agent. Kaboom!

Turn off your phone at your peril. Miss calls and risk losing commissions!

It's basic real estate ABC to respond to clients straight away, but you would be surprised how many buyers have told me that they have not received call-backs from other agents. All the latest technology in the world won't make up for that fact.

Be response-able: it will make you stand out from the crowd, show you are a great communicator and gain clients' respect. In my view, you are in the game 150%: if not, don't bother and shut this book now. Sorry – no refunds!

"

# You were always communicative and enthusiastic, and your performance backed up your word'

–A seller's perspective

# KEY THREE

---

## Connect with your PEOPLE

# Chapter Ten

# Love Sellers

Clients typically dislike hard-hitting real estate agents. That's why my 'soft touch' philosophy served me well. My obsession is people, a must-have trait for a winning property agent! I am not sure whether it's politically correct to use 'soft touch' and 'stupid' in the same sentence, but let's just say it anyway: the soft touch translates to 'focus on the people, stupid'!

It's never about the property. A modest studio or a penthouse, it does not matter. Any property sells at a price. It's about dealing with the emotions of everyone involved—not just the sellers or the buyers, but all the stakeholders, who will test your stamina and people skills.

In real estate, we work exclusively for the seller, however we also deal with the demands of competing interested affiliates as well.

A moral compass is the basis for great customer service, living by the well-known saying of 'treat people as you would like to be treated'. Clients gravitate to positive and proactive agents and shy away from the aggressive, superficial kind.

Make all your dealings fun and fair, and be respectful to people from all walks of life. Be kind to everyone from the cleaner you meet in the lift, to the first home buyer or the penthouse owner.

Besides, there is a high possibility that in some way, the buyer, tenant or affiliate you work with today will become your client down the track, either personally or through friends and family they refer you to.

So, let's dive into the people business...

### Soft touch

How do sellers choose an agent? Various research shows that about 50% of sellers pick their agents by referral through family or friends. Sellers demand excellent service, and the real estate agent who is known for providing off-the-chart professional assistance will be called on and will consequently build a successful referral business.

Start by being different! Add a personal touch to everything. Show small gestures of compassion, like bringing some flowers along to a meeting with a prospective seller who told you they are going through a rough time; or gifting fresh fruit from the markets or a few coffee vouchers to tenants, compensating for the inconvenience of Saturday open houses. Ensure all gestures are something thoughtful.

Channel Mother Theresa in all your interactions, tap into your inner soft touch, and build a reputation for doing the right thing!

## Marketing fees

Another avenue where you can be different is in the marketing of a property. Add your own creativity with targeted e-bulletins to the database, off-market promotions, professional flyers, additional twilight inspections, social media ads, personal contacts, and 'unit caravans' for buyers (taking several buyer groups to a selection of similar properties).

However, the media to use for any successful sale, whilst extremely costly, are web portals, where you share your own advertisement on a host website designed for marketing.

"

# A business absolutely devoted to service will have one worry about profits. They will be embarrassingly large.'

– Henry Ford, Ford Motor Company

There are plenty of real estate courses teaching agents how to convince clients to part with their money and fund their own marketing campaigns. Agents even receive awards for bringing in the highest advertising dollars.

Understandably, sellers are reluctant to spend up big on advertising fees, faced with the uncertainty that the sale may not happen, and fees may be used to boost the agent's profile instead. Most clients want to keep this cost at an absolute minimum.

Despite this, the prices for sales advertisements on web portals have risen sharply over recent years. Some online companies have built up a large market share and therefore are able to increase their fees each year. Increases occur not by the standard Consumer Price Index (CPI rose by 1.9% in the December quarter of 2022: Source - Australian Bureau of Statistics), but generally by a whopping 10-20%.

Agents are compelled to use this form of advertising in their marketing plans for sellers because competitors are doing the same, and clients, conditioned by market forces, expect them as well. It's a vicious cycle that causes the cost for advertisements on web portals perpetually to rise.

It's a no-win situation for agents who one day soon will be replaced altogether by the internet portals. Or that's the game plan, but I am convinced that won't happen as even the best AI software can't deal with the level of emotion that real estate presents.

As I watched the prices of advertisements escalate year in and year out, I came to a point where I could not justify passing on these costs to my clients anymore. I took a chance and opted to go against what all other agents, namely my competitors, were doing. I stuck with the most cost-effective basic subscription on the web portals, rather than opting to pay up big for premium ads (like everyone else in my BDA).

This was a huge gamble on my part, as I knew my competition would be all over it like a rash, using this against me in listing presentations with sellers as soon as the news was out. Marketing companies and some agents will argue that a better price is achieved with bigger ads.

I don't believe this to be true, at least not for all markets, and not for active agents who have a substantial presence in their BDA. In my view, marketing lots of similar listings and working with a large database provides sufficient lead generation for each additional property to be sold. The proof was in the pudding for me, as referrals and sales had increased after the 12 months of my trial. The only downside I faced was having to counteract aggressive agents by educating prospective sellers a little more on their selling options.

In essence, I saved each of my clients thousands of dollars in advertising fees.

## Presenting a property for sale

Rule number one in presenting a property for sale is to keep the décor as neutral as possible. Sellers need to be coached diplomatically (a foreign concept for Germans—'Seller X, what were you sinking?') to change, declutter, and redecorate their property if necessary. It must be appealing to the widest range of buyers and so create the greatest interest, which ultimately will result in a higher price.

I have come across bright green master bedrooms, nude artwork (I mean really nude), and too many pieces of house furniture squashed into a small space of an apartment. Then there is the lack of cleanliness in tenanted units, where the seller may be asked to arrange for a cleaner prior to each open house.

I remember listing a house for sale on a sought-after street in my BDA. It had been on the market before with another local agent. The seller was lovely, but it was a tough one as he had covered most walls of the house with huge religious pictures. And there was an altar in every room.

As a good Catholic girl, I found the life-size Jesus staring at me at every move quite intimidating, and I was sure some of my buyers would feel the same.

I tactfully managed to convince this owner to remove some of the larger artifacts. Even then, the atmosphere in the house was very intense. Every inspection was a reminder of my sins and that I hadn't seen the inside of a church for a long time. Was it a sign?

Dianne, a buyer, was keen to inspect and on arrival told me straight out that she was dealing with the previous agent but didn't like her. I thanked her for disclosing that, and thought that could spell trouble.

I established a good rapport with Dianne and her husband, and showed them through the property a few times before negotiating the sale. At the same time, to protect myself I checked with the Real Estate Institute of Queensland (REIQ) to confirm that I was not doing the wrong thing. I wasn't! I was the agent effecting the sale, and I was entitled to the commission. I was able to defend myself when I, not unexpectedly, received a horrid phone call from the other agent.

## Contract conditions - cooling off

Once a contract is signed, the seller needs to be kept informed until the deposit has been paid, the five-day cooling-off period has past, and all special conditions have been satisfied. It's important to keep promoting the property and provide feedback to the seller until the contract has become unconditional. Additional work for the agent, yes, but should the contract fall over, it provides a smooth transition to restart the sales process instead of losing the listing to another agent.

At another time, I had signed a contract achieving close to the asking price for an upmarket two-bed apartment. I now explained the special conditions and cooling off period to Nigel, the seller. Then he started to become emotional and complained loudly, 'It's all in the buyer's favour! And subject to body corporate searches! On top of that, they have a 5-day cooling off period! Do I get a cooling off period?'

Deflecting his rage, I said, 'Yes, you do! You can go and have a cold shower!' We both laughed.

The job of a real estate agent is to manage expectations, and be completely honest and upfront with all parties involved. I always reassured my clients, urging them to relax and to let me worry about the sale – and I genuinely did. Feedback to sellers is important, some-times daily (for high maintenance clients), but mostly weekly. Keeping clients well-informed is paramount. I desired to achieve the best result possible and put my heart and soul into every sale.

One of my more astute clients once commented that out there in the marketplace, I was known for achieving the best prices and 'buyers beware'! He then said, 'Hannah I will sell with you, but not buy from you.' And that encapsulates what it means to love your sellers!

# Chapter Eleven

# Love Buyers

With twenty thousand people on my database, it's fair to say I have worked with every buyer personality you can imagine. To simplify, I have characterised four distinct purchaser profiles:

1. The efficient buyer
2. The emotional buyer
3. The experienced buyer
4. The energetic buyer

### The efficient buyer

This group are the engineers, quantity surveyors, accountants and even first home buyers. These individuals conduct a lot of research and demand detail, statistics, forecasts, and other information. They take considerable time before making a buying decision. You spot them easily as they are carrying spreadsheets and taking notes, particularly regarding financials, and examining in depth the data provided.

To illustrate, I arranged a showing with Fred, an engineer, who had already researched for months prior to meeting with me, and yes, he clutched a clipboard with his worksheet. Fred ended up buying a property from one of my competitors, based purely on numbers and return on investment. I was unsuccessful in asking him to factor in the floor plan, size of apartment and longevity of the view, as well as rent returns, which can vary anyway due to market forces. No, he did not listen and it broke my heart when I saw that Fred's property sold a few years later at a loss.

## The emotional buyer

These are the divorcees, people changing states due to job transfers, victims of natural disasters like floods, or people going through other life upheavals.

Buyers in this group are going through a dramatic time in their lives and are highly charged. They require calm reassurance and guidance to find the best solution for them. These buyers need a lot of handholding and assistance to make the buying process as easy as possible for them. Suggestions, depending on the buyer's risk profile, could be, for example, to consider purchasing a large one-bed with study unit instead of spending $100,000 more for a two-bedroom apartment. It can be wise to advise the buyer to talk with their accountant, to check the best option and that they are not overextending themselves. Alternatively, depending on the rental market, I have now and then suggested to these buyers to perhaps rent first for a few months whilst doing research.

The emotional buyers will commonly bring family members, friends, or work colleagues along for a second opinion. This often leads to a lot of objections about why the property shouldn't be bought. It is a practice in some cultures for the whole family to join an inspection to pick out all the negative attributes of the property: if the buyer still wants to buy after that, then it's the right decision. I must admit this practice caused me high anxiety on numerous occasions over the years.

Knowing how to overcome objections distinguishes the good agent from the bad. When the buyer first enters a property, some agents are known to aggressively vomit up all the reasons why this is the absolute best property on the market! Even so, the buyer may have decided at first sight that the property may not be for them. A better approach is to authentically listen to the purchaser's needs, gently reinforce the attributes of the property, and if appropriate, provide solid information and establish whether another listing may be more suitable.

It is important to stay neutral whilst supportive, especially with divorcees who are often wrapped up in emotions and are anxious to move forward. This is where experienced agents shine, and can instil the confidence the buyer needs to put pen to paper.

### The experienced buyer

These are the 'mum and dads' and experienced investors. They know what they want and are happy to listen to the agent's opinions and advice. They have typically had property dealings before. They may be purchasing the second or third investment property or buying a place for the university kids.

I once inspected a unit in the city with a lovely Japanese lady, Jocelyn, who was looking to purchase for her son, as he was starting at the Queensland University of Technology. The unit was nicely presented. Then I noticed that the well-meaning tenant, a public servant, had left his laptop screen open, sitting on the bedside table. The screen did not go into sleep mode and neither did his generous private parts on display in all their glory. I was torn between closing the lid and NOT touching my tenant's private parts... I mean property. I decided on the latter and let nature take its course. I was nervously waiting for a reaction from Jocelyn. As she left the bedroom, she exhibited a huge smile on her face. IT sealed the deal.

## The energetic buyer

These are the solicitors, company directors and managers. By nature, they are time-poor, fast-moving and goal-oriented: they come, see and conquer. The agent must be prepared with all the facts or get squashed like a bug.

On a different note, be careful, too, of buyers telling you that it will be an easy sale. Generally, as soon as those words are uttered you know it won't be. But easy sales do happen! Like that day Antonio, a businessman from Spain, viewed an apartment with a great river view in the Brisbane CBD. He stepped onto the balcony and within seconds, turned around and said with a broad Spanish accent, 'I BUY!' The contract was signed and settled in record time. Olé olé olé!

## Buyer criteria

Buyers get frustrated when the agent shows them what seem to be totally inappropriate listings. Truth be told, most people think they know what they like, but then fall in love with a particular aspect of a property, like a stunning view or extra granny flat, and all other criteria go out the window.

Even though the buyers' requirements stipulated that they didn't want a house on a steep block, a noisy road, or on train lines, that may be exactly what they buy. At the moment of truth—the point where the buyer has become emotionally involved and approves the property—there is nothing else to be said. They can see themselves living there; or they believe it would be a great addition to their investment portfolio. That's when they pull out the tape measure or mention how they would furnish the property.

Don't hesitate at that moment; close the deal by asking the buyer for a decision. Depending on their risk profile, ask one of the following questions: 'Can I email you an Expression of Interest form?' 'Would you like to make an offer?' 'Would you like me to provide you with a draft contract?' 'Would you like me to prepare a contract?'.

Consistency is the key in dealing with buyer enquiries. I am still surprised every time I hear in conversation with a buyer that I was the only one who had responded to their inquiry. I suggest bending over backward for potential buyers! A buyer today is a seller tomorrow.

# Chapter Twelve

# Love Affiliates

You don't want to get on the wrong side of your affiliates, for obvious reasons. These are the rainmakers; they can make or break a deal. Excellent communication with this group, the valuers, building inspectors, finance brokers, solicitors, body corporate managers, and building and property managers, is mandatory.

### Etiquette dealing with affiliates

*Rule number one:* Be of service by providing requested information promptly, and ideally, before being asked. This can include documents like a dated contract, a title search, a rental appraisal, brochures, a list of supportive sales data, or floor plans.

*Rule number two*: Be friendly and greet affiliates with a strong handshake. An enjoyable meeting will result in better outcomes.

*Rule number three*: Be punctual and upbeat for any appointment. It will keep your affiliates happy, especially valuers, who are notoriously time poor. It is sacrilege letting a valuer wait. (It could result in a lower valuation and potentially crash a deal.)

*Rule number four*: Go the extra mile. This can include specifying directions to the property, entry to the building, the height of the garage door, or organising a free visitor car park, important in a metropolitan area.

*Rule number five*: Follow up. Ensure all parties have received documents they need and gently coach things along to settlement.

## Valuers

Valuations are part and parcel of any property trans-action. Making things as easy as possible for valuers is essential. Don't keep them waiting. Provide them with parking, a copy of the contract, rental appraisal, floor and carpark plans, a summary of building attributes, and comparable sales. Nice gestures are offering chocolates, assisting with any of their other valuations, and discussing the market. Acknowledge that you understand they get paid very little for what they do, hence time is money, and they prefer to be in and out in the shortest possible time.

On a side note, if there is a furniture package included in the sale price, organise for the buyer's solicitor and accountant to check options regarding a special condition for the contract, to reflect the value. This is important, as otherwise the valuation may be lower than the contract price because a certain amount may be deducted for the furniture package and the buyer consequently may not be able to secure the finance.

Organising property valuations can be tricky. In one case, I made multiple phone calls and sent multiple emails and succeeded in rearranging a few bookings for a serviced apartment (a property that is let on a short-term basis by the on-site manager). The challenge was to organise an appointment for a valuation of a dual-key apartment – a property with a main entry and then two separate entrances, in this case, one leading into a one-bed unit and the other into a studio.

I was so grateful that I was able to gain access, as it is nigh on impossible to have both sides of a dual-key apartment available at the same time; a real problem that frequently delays finance approvals. Swiping us into the one-bed unit, the valuer had a quick look around. I then casually opened the door to the studio. Normally, as a matter of principal, I would knock first, but not this time. Whoops. We were greeted by Adonis in his underwear. Panicking, I knew I absolutely needed to finish this valuation. God only knows when the stars would align once more and both parts of this dual key unit would be available again.

I chatted calmly and asked if it would be okay to show a valuer through for just a couple of minutes. Shell-shocked, the guest replied, 'Can I at least put some clothes on first?' The female valuer then zipped through the unit in seconds and the buyer's finance was approved within a few days.

## Building managers

When handling apartment sales, the building manager is your friend. It is vital to establish a good rapport and keep in close communication to ensure smooth inspections and deal with any building-related issues that may arise. Generally, building managers are suspicious of agents as their concern is that business (as in property management clients) will be taken away from them.

Most agents also operate a property management business themselves, and once they sell a property to an investor, they take over the management. Or if the property is currently tenanted and an owner-occupier buys, then the management would be lost as well. Either way, managers are not happy when apartments are listed for sale, and some make it difficult for the agents to conduct their inspections for that reason.

I was in the fortunate position of specialising in sales only, and referred business back to the on-site building managers. Nevertheless, I had my fair share of resistance from some of them. Remember, I said before: one sent me a lawyer's letter trying to stop me handing out chocolates to reception staff.

## Agents

Liaising with other agents can be tricky. I must admit, most agents made me feel uncomfortable and I found it difficult to connect. Certainly, I do know agents I would trust, but they are a rarity. I experienced plenty of incidents that made me cautious about collaborating.

I suffered through a few 'conjunctions' with various agents during my career. A conjunction happens when another agent introduces a buyer to a property you are listing, and the argument is that the seller will ultimately obtain a better price as there is additional competition. The downside is that the listing agent is not in control of what the other agent discloses to potential purchasers. The facts, including price expectations, can be misconstrued, leading to problems later.

Then there are the phone calls from agents pretending to be buyers. These unethical agents brazenly call from their office and make the inquiry. I find that not only extremely insulting to my intelligence but also disappointing. I also frequently had other agents turn up 'coincidently' at the same time as my open houses or individual inspections were arranged during the week.

In high-rise apartment buildings, there are approximately 10-15% of properties for sale at any given time. If some other agents had units for sale in the same building as my advertised opens, they would place their *For Sale* signs in front of the entrance, next to mine, and attempt to snatch a 'hot buyer'.

Once, such a competitor came along and set up his sign next to mine. I questioned him: 'Were the Courier Mail advertisements (*I am showing my age here*) and internet listings I placed and paid for big enough for you?'

He replied, 'But everyone is doing it!'

I sharply retorted, 'That doesn't make it right!' Incensed, with steam coming out of my ears and our faces almost touching, I challenged him: 'Do you want to take it outside?'

I guess it was the straw that broke the camel's back.

I learned to live with unethical behaviour in the industry for over twenty years, and concede, 'Children, violence is never the answer'! Unfortunately, until there is a meaningful emphasis on a code of ethics in real estate, monitored by the appropriate regulatory bodies, I can't see a change happening in the foreseeable future.

"

# There may be times when we are powerless to prevent injustice, but there must never be a time when we fail to protest.'

– Elie Wiesel

# KEY FOUR

---

## PRICE matters — but it's not everything

# Chapter Thirteen

# Market Appraisals

Everything is about the price. It begins with a comparative market analysis (CMA) when appraising a property's value, based on similar sales in the BDA area.

Providing market appraisals to prospective sellers is a great tool to help you not only stay in touch with them, but primarily to secure listings. Accuracy is the key to taking all property attributes into account and checking facts carefully. Best practice is to incorporate a checklist, so nothing is missed. The seller typically provides all the finer details like inclusions in a furniture package, status on existing leases, or an extra carpark purchased, which may not have shown up on the property data online portals.

On a separate note, when a seller owns and offers a furniture package as part of the unit sale, ensure this is stated on the Form 6 sales agreement to avoid any confusion when a contract is signed. I learned this the hard way. A seller had verbally confirmed that the furniture was included, which was then corrected by the on-site manager just before settlement, long after the contract was signed. Thank goodness, in this case, the buyer wasn't worried. This could have potentially crashed the deal and ended up in a dispute. The lesson learned – document all conversations and reconfirm via email.

Frequently, investors request market appraisals without having to disturb the tenants. Experienced agents are very much across values and don't need to inspect the property. It's a straightforward process of simply checking recent sales and historical transactions from online data providers.

Estimating the property value is one thing, but it takes a skilled agent to convince a potential seller that the price suggestion is accurate, and to prepare the client for agents who promise a higher price.

The fact is that sellers' price expectations are commonly 5-10% above market value, enticing some agents to quote a higher price to 'buy the listing', which is a term used too often in the property industry.

I would specify a price range that I believed to be realistic for the prevailing market conditions. Being truthful with market appraisals lost me plenty of opportunities in my career. Conversely, I developed a reputation for giving honest advice. Clients could trust the information and consequently make good decisions. I would also receive requests for market appraisals by referrals: 'You sold Philip's place a few months ago and he said you would provide us with a no BS appraisal, and that's what we want!'

How do you counteract an unethical inflated market appraisal from another agent? Communicate, communicate, and communicate some more!

Ongoing relationships with potential sellers are critical. Stay in touch with sales successes, market updates, and sales reports for similar products. Provide rental and market appraisals and just have a friendly chat now and then. Sellers are then more likely to trust you and request your opinion when considering the best time to place their property on the market and the list price.

Nevertheless, some sellers couldn't resist choosing the agent who suggested a market price that matched their price expectation, and would justify that with things like, 'Oh sorry, we gave the listing to the other agent as they believe in the value of our property'.

What could I say to that, when there was hard evidence that similar units sold for 10-20% less? 'Well, thank you for letting me know. Good luck with the sale, but please be in touch should things not work out.'

The sad part is that in the end, such a seller would often accept a much lower price than the one I quoted. There is lots of similar anecdotal evidence of what happens when a seller engages the agent who gives them the highest estimated price.

For example, a seller signed the Form 6 sales agreement, and the agent left and drove away. Shortly after, the agent called the seller from the car and admitted, 'Sorry, I made a mistake. I now think your property is worth X'. Typically, a sales agreement stands for 90 days and in that situation, there was not much the seller could do!

In other situations, sellers are presented with low verbal offers in the first week after listing the property at an agent's inflated value.

A seller's high expectation of price with another agent has regularly resulted in a property being sold for much less than the amount I quoted to them in my appraisals. Why? Because most buyer interest happens in the first few weeks of the marketing period. If the property is overpriced, then no one makes offers in that time. As there are a certain number of buyers for a specific product in the market at any given time, it takes months for fresh buyers to come into the market. That's why, even if the price is reduced and reduced again, this generally doesn't excite the existing purchasers. If anything, they query what is wrong with the property. Usually, after months of sitting on the market, the sellers' circumstances are such that they must accept a low offer.

On the flipside, some sellers who held out for the three months of unsuccessful marketing with another agent came back to me. They then set a realistic price, and the property usually sold fairly quickly. This was, of course, due to the first agent presenting low offers and providing plenty of feedback from buyers in regard to the price.

Anecdotal evidence suggest that some unethical agents engage in the practice of 'conditioning the seller'. This entails presenting fictious verbal low offers early on in the marketing to counter the agents overpriced market appraisal, as well as to encourage the seller to accept an offer earlier.

The code of ethics in real estate stipulates pricing a property according to current market value based on research into comparable properties. 'Do not deceive sellers by inflating the price or giving out misleading information'. The agent's estimated selling price must be realistic.

Solid research needs to be undertaken to support any market appraisal. No shortcuts! Experience and extensive knowledge of the market are essential to confidently set the price of a property correctly every time. This expertise will shine through in conversations with the seller.

My preferred sales strategy is based on a fixed price, setting the list price slightly above market value, and then achieving the full price or close to it. That way, various offers are received quickly.

This tactic can cause some sellers anxiety because they think the price must be too cheap if they receive multiple offers quickly. I always explained that the price has to be competitive in the prevailing market. Receiving multiple offers pushes up the price as opposed to waiting for the right buyer to offer a high price.

A similar pricing option is to list a price and invite offers, generally using the minimum price a seller would accept, as in: 'Offers invited from $X.' This often leads to multiple offers early in the marketing campaign, and this competition results in buyers offering higher to a point. That point, of course, is where a purchaser perceives a similar property in the market as better value.

The agent must provide feedback to the seller, explaining that buyer X can buy property X for a lower price than theirs, and list the attributes of that property, which may have an extra study, be larger in size, have a better view, or additional storage, for example.

With years of experience and confidence comes opportunity. An existing client, Mark, who had previously sold a property with me, once requested a market appraisal for his late mum's riverfront penthouse. This was an extremely saleable property! As I had already gained Mark's trust, he asked me to list the property straight away at the price I recommended. He also accepted the advertising fees for the marketing program without question.

Establishing a reputation for providing honest market appraisals drove my success, and I frequently sold the same property two or three times to consecutive buyers.

"

# It takes 20 years to build a reputation and five minutes to ruin it. If you think about that, you'll do things differently.'

– Warren Buffett

# Chapter Fourteen

# Auction Lessons

Sellers can choose the method of sale for their property. There are various options, including auction, tender/ expression of interest, and private treaty. Each sale method has pros and cons in terms of achieving the optimal price.

A private treaty sale is the most common option. This gives buyers a price indication, whilst auctions are generally suited for up-market or unique properties. In general, buyers don't like to consider properties without a price tag.

## Auctions

Most agencies promote auctions as the best way to sell a property. Agents believe they can achieve the best price in the shortest possible time, and of course, everyone gets paid sooner.

The sellers' advertising and marketing fees are generally higher for auctions. The short marketing campaign ensures the seller is educated instantly on the real market price.

Depending on market conditions and property type, prices achieved can be both above and below market value.

When starting out in my career, Heath, the sales manager, kindly handed me a couple of townhouses owned by one seller so I could take them through auction programs under his supervision. They were not located in my business development area, but he saw it as an opportunity for me to learn the ropes. The seller, Connor, was a kind-hearted man who had agreed to our marketing campaign and paid thousands of dollars in upfront fees.

The townhouses were in an estate, and similar new developments were being established nearby. Being at the tail end of a quiet market was also a negative in terms of sales potential. However, it was an opportunity for me to learn the sales system of the auction method, to communicate with buyers, and to provide feedback to Connor.

The four-week marketing campaign flew by, with very little response from the market. Unsurprisingly, my stress levels went up as the auction day fast approached. Then Heath and I had the pre-auction chat with Connor to set the reserve price. His defensive body language showed he was not impressed. He had parted with a substantial amount of marketing monies, only for me to tell him that there may be only a couple of buyers interested, if that; and that unless he adjusted his price, the expectation was that the properties wouldn't sell.

The atmosphere was tense: you could hear a pin drop and I felt extremely uneasy. I had a bad conscience, and I didn't blame him for being slightly angry. Due to the limited response, the reserve was set low with the aim of achieving a result on the day.

I had sleepless nights leading up to the auction day. Heath had instructed me to hire a crowd, as in, bring in friends and anyone I could pick up off the street to make up an audience. The crowd activity is meant to show any prospective buyer that the property is worth bidding on. I had a few friends then, but all of them were agents who had their own open houses on Saturdays.

I set my doubts aside and desperately, as a last resort, placed directional signs… lots of them… around the streets near the property, in the hope of attracting a few more buyers to the auction.

Auction day finally came. The first of a handful of auctions I have ever orchestrated was in full swing. The auctioneer was doing his thing and working the small assembly… 'calling once, twice and'… shock, horror… the properties were passed in, one after the other. No sale. I was traumatised and made a mental note to avoid auctions at all costs.

Would these properties have achieved better prices if they were sold by private treaty? I will never know.

A couple of months later, I eventually sold the town-houses and learned two lessons.

- Lesson one, stick to your BDA, as marketing efforts outside of it don't grow your business.
- Lesson two, just because auctions are accepted practice by many agencies, it doesn't make it a good option for all property sales.

Later in my career, when people asked me why I didn't handle auctions, I bared all: 'Auctions are absolute pressure cookers! Why would anyone ever consider this nerve-wracking experience, when everybody, including the seller, the buyer and the agent, is stressed out?'

In my view, auctions only work in a buzzing sellers' market, or for exclusive or unique properties. Personally, I prefer to sell properties by private treaty, as at times it takes longer to find that premium buyer.

My philosophy has always been to keep a seller well-informed and only recommend price reductions when necessary. If the seller asked me to persevere with the current list price even if it meant it took a lot longer to sell, that was fine too.

Some online internet portals report the number of 'days on market' for properties, with a short time obviously being a benefit. Although, a higher number of 'days on market' could just mean that those agents are not forcing their client to accept low offers.

# Chapter Fifteen

# Negotiate the Deal

When it comes to the crunch, the deal must get done. The first step is to reflect the asking price appropriately to the buyer. Do not underquote the price; rather, convince the buyer to make a decent offer by promoting the benefits of the property.

Provide recent sales and supportive statistics and take the time to go through all intricacies of the property. Agents equipped with 150% knowledge of the marketplace can easily counter any objections thrown up by buyers.

Legally, agents are not allowed to disclose what price the seller is hoping to achieve or what level other offers are at. However, agents can ensure offers begin at a realistic amount by gently pushing for them to be in the realm of the seller's expectations.

Here are a few tips for effective negotiations:

## 1.   Know the facts

What are the benefits of the property and why is the price justified? Do your homework and research everything there is to know about the listing, like owner's timing; price expectations; lease details; historical sales; competitive listings; existing and future infrastructure; and, possible improvements that could be made to the property and associated costings. Have supporting documents ready, like depreciation schedules and title encumbrances.

When selling a unit, know the ratio between owners and investors, and whether it is a residential or serviced apartment. Serviced apartments are furnished units available for short-term or long-term stays, which most banks class as riskier investments. This black-and-white rule makes it more challenging for buyers to obtain finance.

It is a good idea to keep in touch with a mortgage broker to be well-informed about lending guidelines. A buyer may well say, 'I have preapproval with X bank'; however, the bank will conduct a valuation before approving the loan. One of the first questions a valuer will ask is 'Is it a serviced apartment?' Some banks only lend 70% on a serviced apartment, rather than the typical 80% of a purchase price. For such a property worth $500,000, a buyer would have to provide an extra $50,000, an amount that not everyone has lying around.

In addition, once a bank has invested a certain level in a building, they will stop lending to other buyers there, to manage their exposure to risk. Therefore, buyers should be encouraged to apply for a mortgage with multiple financial institutions.

In short, ensure you're prepared for all scenarios and leave no doubt in a buyer's mind that this is the best property they can find.

## 2. Personal brand

An agent who has developed a positive personal brand will be more memorable, and importantly, will invoke action.

A personalised professional dress code influences people positively in a sales environment. Any dishevelled look in your presentation, tardiness, or disorganisation will reflect badly on your dealings with buyers. It could also place the property in a bad light and make purchasers subconsciously question what is wrong with it.

Incidentally, if you like to give yourself the edge in negotiations, wear something red. Research suggests red triggers nervous system arousal and stimulates excitement and action. It can enhance persuasiveness. As a rule, I would wear something red or complement my outfit with a red laptop bag or similar. Red heightens emotions and power, and signals action to clients in negotiations!

### 3.   Ask for the offer

Once it is established that the buyer is interested, it's simply a matter of asking for the order. 'Would you like to make an offer on this fabulous property?' Don't wait for the buyer to make a move!

Typically, the purchaser responds, 'What do you think a good offer would be?'

I would reply, 'Well, I suggest giving it a good shot and I will try my best for you!'

I negated lower offers with phrases like, 'The seller's preferred number for the price starts with a 5' when, for example, the buyer offered $495,000. Or 'The seller is hoping for an offer closer to the asking price. Would you be prepared to offer more?'

Buyers sometimes told me in inspections that a rival agent told them they could buy a similar property for X amount. Then, when the buyer makes the offer at that price level, negotiations drag on and the agent tells the buyer that the seller is not getting back to them, or is outright refusing the offer.

This tactic of 'baiting a buyer' entices the buyer to make an offer by quoting a low price and implying the seller may accept it. The motive is to get the buyer hooked and then eventually mediate the deal at a higher price. This sneaky approach is to be avoided, as it generally disappoints all parties involved, and will not help an agent's reputation.

By law, agents need to present all offers to the seller, even though it may be well below the asking price and the agent is already aware that it won't be accepted. I would document these in my weekly feedback to the seller, describing them as a verbal offer made by a bargain hunter.

It is important to not get the seller offside. Emphasise that you don't expect them to accept a lowball offer. Good rapport with the seller will be critical at a later stage, during more serious negotiations. But don't dismiss these offers altogether, as I have negotiated them successfully on a few occasions.

## 4.  Be flexible

Consider all options when discussing a potential contract with the buyer and seller. What will move this deal over the line? Often the parties may be only a few thousand dollars apart. Think outside the square.

For example, the property may have been advertised as fully furnished. In conversation, the seller may disclose that they may like to keep the furniture after all, whilst the buyer has his own and doesn't really want it. Excluding it from the contract could seal the deal.

Or the buyer may be agreeable to letting the seller rent back for a couple of months at no cost. The possibilities are endless. I once had a sale where I reallocated a carpark in a community title scheme, obtaining approval from the body corporate first and then changing a Community Management Statement (CMS) through solicitors. (A CMS is a significant document that sets out the rules for a particular building as per the body corporate scheme.)

Carparks in high-rise buildings are commonly not on the title of each property, but are allocated for exclusive use of residents. That exclusive right can generally only be changed if 100% of the owners in the building consent, including the seller.

## 5. Take the time

Invest time: there is nothing more important to do than bring the buyer and the seller closer to finalising the deal and preparing a contract for sale.

Listen to all concerns and go over everything carefully, repeating back to both sides what was said, for example: 'Buyer X, I understand you currently have a lease that finishes in three months' time. Would you increase your offer by X amount, if I can get the seller to agree to a longer settlement?' In this scenario, the purchaser avoids paying rent and the mortgage for that period.

Ideally, you would only make this kind of proposition if you knew from prior conversations that the seller would be agreeable.

Ensure you hear out both parties' positions and make your moves accordingly, just like a chess player.

## 6. Stay in communication

Stay in close contact with everyone until the deal is done. Follow up with phone calls to check each party's position frequently, but don't annoy them: just have a light-hearted conversation. Even if negotiations are at a stalemate, your communications could reveal further information that could bring the groups together. The seller or buyer may throw up a solution the agent has not thought of.

Persevere with checking if the buyer could increase their offer and, equally, if the seller would consider a further reduction. You could say to the buyer: 'I understand $X was your limit, but you never know. If you could perhaps give me an extra $X, it may just make the difference?' And to the seller: 'We're very close. Would you consider moving by $X?'

During the marketing of a property, similarly priced offers are often received. This sets the benchmark! It is imperative to make that position clear to the seller. For example: 'We have to date shown over 40 groups through the property. We have received three offers at around $X. Here we have an offer of $Y, 5% above that level! This demonstrates it is a good offer and this could be our premium buyer. If you let go of this offer, we may have to wait another few months before we receive a similar offer again, which may or may not happen. But ultimately this is your decision!'

The funny thing about negotiations is that not everything goes to plan, and market conditions do change quickly.

I recall when a particularly slow period of a month had gone by without a sale. The property market had been tough for over 12 months, due to a perfect storm made up of consistent negative press regarding apartment oversupply in Brisbane; tightening of finance for investment properties, in particular interest-only loans; and China restricting overseas property purchases for its citizens.

At last, I negotiated a deal for a 2-bed apartment in the Brisbane CBD. The buyers had made multiple offers and had plenty of choices. I was elated when they decided on mine, and the seller agreed to the offer.

Then came a call the next day from the seller. 'Hannah, my wife doesn't want to sell now!' '*@%?!' I had to disappoint the buyer, and though they didn't blame me, it would have left a bad taste in their mouth, for sure.

Then, a week later, I received four offers on four different apartments. The law of averages told me that I should get at least two or three over the line. Incidentally, this ratio depends very much on how easy it is for a buyer to obtain finance, how cautious valuers are, the number of properties listed for sale, and an array of other market forces.

One of the offers was submitted by Simon, who had made offers on two properties on his shortlist. He submitted $488,000 on my property, where the seller had originally paid $490,000. This seller was keen to sell a few weeks ago but now the reason to sell was no longer there and he didn't want to accept lower than

$490,000. I couldn't push Simon any further because he was already tossing up between this and another unit. When that happens it's 'some of the pie or nothing', so I negotiated the deal by reducing my fees.

Time is of the essence when presenting offers, as buyers can cool quickly, and circumstances are ever-evolving. Point in case, during the 24 hours of negotiations, Simon's offer on the other property was accepted. He was now in a predicament and wanted to consider his options over the weekend. I was philosophical but when Simon emailed me on Monday morning to tell me that he wanted to proceed with my listing, I was over the moon.

Lesson – don't count your chickens until they have hatched… or the contract is signed and has become unconditional. Very rarely, only once or twice during my whole career, did a settlement (when all the money is handed over and the property transfers to the buyer) not take place.

The reasons for such devastating events can be varied. Perhaps the seller's bank doesn't want to settle due to the existing loan being linked to another property, which has been valued lower than expected. Other reasons could be that estate or divorce settlements have gone wrong. When this happens there is only one thing left to do – get out the ice cream.

In property dealings, sometimes completely reasonable people display irrational behaviour. I remember one discussion about a million-dollar house contract. Neville, the seller, was prepared to lose the sale over a $200 repair bill to fix the knob on a dishwasher.

In negotiating a property sale, creativity is key. Determine what is of advantage to either party and adapt that into the transaction. Outstanding real estate agents are diplomatic and stay calm and in control in all communications. Think win-win!

Every sale achieved is as thrilling as the next one, especially when the market is buzzing—it becomes highly addictive. I punched the air in excitement every time an intense negotiation wrapped up with a contract signed.

"

# We are very grateful for the way that you have kept us informed every step of the way and your fair and pragmatic approach to bringing negotiations to resolution.'

– Seller

# KEY FIVE

## The subtle art of the PUSH

# Chapter Sixteen

# Mindset

'Push through the pain barrier', coupled with a fist bump, became one of my many mantras—similar to Lleyton Hewitt's irritating 'Come on'—that helped me stay focused on my goals when things got tough. I became my own inner task master, driving the next sale, and ultimately, an entire successful sales career. That, and a few other things I learned along the way.

Think, dancing to the tune of Tina Turner's 'Nutbush City Limits'. Stay with me here... seriously, if you have the energy to dance through that song to the end, then I suggest a career in real estate is for you.

**"**

# The best way out is always through.'

– Robert Frost

## Vision board

Take organised action. It all starts with a vision board – a physical display of your goals (or a screensaver on a laptop if you must), placed in a prominent place where you can glance at it daily.

A vision board is a constant reminder of your 'why' and helps you avoid procrastination as it subconsciously shapes your thoughts and behaviours. Be elaborate and specific with words, images and photos. Be very clear on what you would like to achieve within one, three and five years. Discover your reason. What does your abundant life look like?

*Oprah Daily* illustrates this with, 'It's wholly possible to turn your dreams into reality. It's called manifestation. Well, that and hard work. For success with manifestation, you have to set your intention, believe that it will become a reality, then take *active* steps towards making that abstract idea come to fruition'.

What are the active steps to becoming a top real estate agent?

## Sports mind

Once your vision board is in a prominent position, your next stop is to prepare your mindset ready for action. Where to start? 'Chunking down your dreams' is the key, explains performance consultant, Jeffrey Hodges B.Sc.(AES) M.Sc.(Hons).

For every thousand people with dreams, only a handful ever bring them into reality. How do they do it? Hodges says by just:

1.  Committing to their dream – by deciding to do it
2.  Regularly and consistently imagining achieving it
3.  Turning the dream into specific, focused goals
4.  Establishing a stepwise action plan to make it happen.

Let's try.

First, identify your current abilities, then list the areas you want to improve:

My strengths are:

_____

Areas I want to improve are:

_____

Now ask yourself:

• How/where do I want to be in six months from now?

- How/where do I want to be in twelve months from now?
- How/where do I want to be in three to five years from now?

Now on a sheet of paper, write down your three most important 6 month, 12 month, 3-5 years, and long-term-outcome goals. Set goals in all areas of your life: career goals; financial goals; study goals; sports and exercise, etc.

Take fifteen minutes to do this now.

As you do this now, remember that most people over-estimate what they can practically achieve in a year, yet greatly under-estimate what they can achieve in ten years, or over their lifetime.

Also, you want to set yourself goals that are almost out of reach; goals that require great physical, emotional and mental efforts to achieve. Remember that if you aim for mediocre goals, that's likely what you'll achieve. If you aim for greatness, you may well reach it. But you'll never know your true potential and untapped talents until you really test yourself.

With Jeffrey Hodges' tips in mind, now create a spreadsheet with your goals. Then create the sub-steps you will need to take in chronological order and break down goals into individual tasks. Set a finishing date, so you take responsibility for completion.

A new property agent may decide to work as a personal assistant to a lead agent for a six-month period. Next, their goal may be to become established as an agent within twelve months; then achieve X number of sales and attain top agent status in their BDA within two years, and so on. In addition, add milestones in other aspects of life to the mix, incorporating family, friends, health and fitness, spirituality, professional development, love, and travel.

## Written diary

I am in love with my Stephen R. Covey diary. To me, it is an indispensable tool, almost like a coach joining me on my daily ride. I write in it, by hand. Each page displays an inspirational quote from Stephen R. Covey's 'The 7 Habits of Highly Effective People', providing a step-by-step path to living with fairness, integrity, honesty, and human dignity. It presents an excellent daily reminder to be focussed on your higher vision and endgame, using your time smartly.

Aside from easily looking back at appointments, contact information and other records like sales successes, it is also a handy tool for proof of conversations, which can be important for legal purposes and peace of mind in business.

There are, of course, digital journals available, like Outlook and various apps. Keep in mind, though, that research has shown writing by hand has many advantages, from memorising facts to aiding critical thinking and creativity.

Once you have created an attitude for a goals-driven mindset and you're clear on your aspirations, get organised. But first, look into a mirror and say passionately three times, 'I am awesome!'

# Chapter Seventeen

# Routines

Regular, repeated actions lead to astounding results over time. One of my favourite practices is having a to-do list for everything. Items are written on small pages from multiple note pads. There is ample research that confirms this is a great method to stay on top of things. Better still, it's known to reduce anxiety, improve memory, lift productivity and create a feeling of accomplishment.

## Habits

In my professional life, I routinely prepare a daily to-do list the night before, listing all important tasks first. In real estate, this could have included scheduling a meeting with a seller to list their property for sale, inspections, discussing a rejected offer with a purchaser, contacting a seller for a price reduction, and so on.

Essentially, focus on the tasks that will produce results and make you money, placing those on top of your list. Schedule personal commitments too, like grooming, family leisure activities and sexercise... I mean, exercise.

Growing up in Germany, various German proverbs were imprinted firmly on my brain, like 'Was du heute kannst besorgen, das verschiebe nicht auf morgen', that translates to 'There's no time like the present'. Top that off with an unhealthy dose of perfectionism and I could not bring myself to leave the office until all items were ticked off. I believe pushing that little bit more to gain the edge over competitors, and consequently my assurance in my own abilities over time, led to a perpetual cycle of sales success.

In addition to the daily list, prepare a short and sharp list of the most important primary weekly tasks. These are non-negotiables and central to an efficient sales week. Tick them off on a whiteboard as each one is completed. This sets the stage for a productive week, every week.

The fixed compulsory tasks on my whiteboard included:

1.  Weekly feedback to sellers

Updating clients on the progress of their marketing helps to establish a good relationship, which is invaluable when later negotiating the sale. It leads to honesty with each other, calm conversations, and good outcomes due to the established trust. Staying in touch also ensures sellers' loyalty when other agents come knocking on the door.

2.  Scheduling open houses, inspections, and buyer follow-up

Setting inspection times early in the week is the basis for effective follow-up calls to active purchasers. These are classified on the database as 'A buyers'; these are the 'hot buyers' who are keenly searching for a property. They are classified as 'B' if their purchase is delayed, and 'C' if they have bought a property or are out of the market for other reasons.

When calling the A list, some buyers may request a second inspection for their preferred property. Alternatively, they may request an inspection of one of the properties they haven't seen yet, or ask you to hunt for a specific off-market property.

It's good practice to organise open houses for as many properties as possible, as a greater overall number of contacts will lead to more listings and increased sales.

## 3.  Update online portals

It is essential to update any changes to property information promptly. Load new photos and inspection times instantly, and have presentation materials for inspections ready to go. For example, a 6- or 12-month lease renewal with tenants in a property that is for sale could mean that the property is no longer attractive to an owner-occupier who would want to move in soon. The property's web text then needs to be targeted towards investors and lease details updated.

## 4.  Prepare and schedule weekly e-bulletin to database

Efficient prospecting starts with staying in touch with your database. A good option is committing to a weekly news bulletin with interesting updates relating to your BDA, property industry, and economic and political data. Done well, it will create long-term relationships, go hand in hand with an impeccable reputation and, in my opinion, will outperform all other marketing strategies over time. Incidentally, that's why, in challenging markets, mostly the dinosaurs, i.e. older experienced agents, survive.

All jokes aside, people from interstate and overseas, in particular, appreciate being kept informed, as they feel removed from their investments when living outside Queensland.

Being kept abreast of the market makes people feel connected and valued, and ultimately they feel enough trust has been established to buy more properties or to list their properties for sale. Some of my clients who have been on my database for years comment, 'Hannah, you have been writing to me for years without fail and I can now finally list my property with you'.

Weekly key tasks must be completed in a timely fashion, typically on Mondays, to commence the week with a clean slate, as things can get crazy quickly. Like the time I sold my partner's riverfront apartment. I had arranged a weekday inspection for a couple of buyer groups and simultaneously listed an open house on the internet portals. This caught the eye of an ABC reporter who was scouting for agents to comment on the current property market.

When I received the reporter's call, I committed excitedly to the interview at the property. Then I got nervous; the pressure was on. I was running on schedule, but there was no time to pick up Valium from a chemist.

Shortly after, the station phoned back and told me I was no longer needed. I thought, 'Thank God' and sighed in relief. As I parked my car, the ABC phoned again, asking, 'Would you still be okay to come along?'

My heart racing, I said casually, 'Sure, no problem. See you soon'.

Multiple groups of purchasers were already waiting for me outside the building. I welcomed them quickly and told them that I would just open the apartment and see everyone in a second.

Panicked, I rushed through the place, switched on lights and opened doors, frantically spraying room freshener as I went. Then I opened the fridge door and took a generous sip out of the first bottle of wine I could find. My English partner is still mortified by such distasteful behaviour.

Then the ABC crew arrived, and I invited everyone into the apartment, providing information to the buyers first and showing them through. After all, a sale comes first. Then I performed the interview, which I thought went very well.

That was before the reporter pointed to the cameraman and asked, 'Was the camera on?' He awkwardly said, 'Oh no, sorry. We have to do it again'. I took a deep breath and said, 'Excuse me just a minute', and went back to the kitchen for another glug of wine.

My phone lit up that night with lots of great messages from clients and friends: 'You're a star' and 'Wow! Hollywood will be calling'. It was great publicity, despite my comments being used to underlay reporting on auction results and other state's property markets. Go figure.

## Cashflow & sales targets

Never take your eyes off your money. Stay in control by managing an Excel spreadsheet or app for your cashflow. Record sale contract details, due dates for the deposit, and important special conditions through to settlement date and commission fees.

Record your current personal cash balance, approximate monthly outgoings, and record balance cash available for the following month. Adapt a three-monthly schedule. Add another column for monthly sales targets in numbers and dollars, as sometimes you may have fewer sales but higher commissions. Plus, record your yearly sales goal in numbers to keep you on track.

The discipline of consistency with work schedules is a growth strategy that will weave through the fabric of your everyday work and become a part of who you are.

Taking the time to prepare clear daily, weekly, and monthly to-do lists has saved my bacon over the years. It meant I stayed in control through tumultuous times and worked efficiently, by completing the important tasks first. It kept me moving forward toward my goals.

That was especially true during leaner times when I had to let go of support staff. Then, I was really worried about how I would ever get everything done, sometimes managing all the administration and marketing tasks, and organising the office by myself.

I surprised myself, as things usually went like clockwork, apart from rare occasions when I placed the wrong open house times for a property on the internet portals. Some buyers would tell me, 'Your assistant messed up', and I would agree and apologise with, 'I will give him a good talking to when I get back to the office'.

# Chapter Eighteen

# Focus

Stay ahead of the game! Take action to move forward and get closer to achieving your goals. The satisfaction of finishing tasks will lead to the desire to accomplish even more. The release of endorphins experienced when each job is completed will strengthen your resolve.

Always work ahead. Be disciplined. For example, when listing a new property, take the time to prepare all associated paperwork, from brochures, information booklets, marketing, expression of interest forms, and disclosure statements to preparing the contract.

You want to be ready when the opportunity for a sale presents itself. There is nothing worse than missing an opportunity to list another property, or being unable to deal with any other demands whilst preoccupied with paperwork. In other words, get organised.

Develop a production-line approach for all your systems and work processes. This leads to increased productivity and efficiencies. Reliability in service performance is cherished by customers and creates return and referral business. This can only be achieved by being always ahead of what needs to be done. Make a point to finish the to-do list daily, come hell or high water.

### The 80 / 20 rule

Focus on the things that will make you the most money. The principle is that only 20% of agents make 80% of the money, and the same applies to 20% of the product you choose to sell as well.

The trick is to figure out which properties will give you the highest return. This may not be just the most expensive units or houses, but could be a niche market, for example, that will reap the best rewards.

For instance, I specialised in a particular high-rise building in the Brisbane CBD that regularly realised the highest percentage of my turnover.

Don't fluff around with inconsequential tasks. Be clear about the essential jobs and focus on those. For instance, don't get bogged down with administration to a point where non-productive work becomes more important than interacting with clients.

There are plenty of interruptions on top of the daily workload: a tenant wanting reassurance regarding the sale of the property; a buyer's bank arranging a valuation or requesting a rental appraisal; buyers having second thoughts; sellers changing the goal post regarding the list price due to another agent exaggerating the value. Then there is the minefield of contract management, dealing with solicitors, finance issues and building inspections gone wrong.

In business today, one of the biggest distractions is technology. Avoid going down the rabbit hole of mindlessly scrolling online, and use your time wisely. Productivity is constantly hampered by email, phone calls and message overload. The idea is to focus on the 20% of tasks that will give the greatest results.

You can never do everything. Though sticking to the completion of your daily plan is imperative, prospecting is the topmost important task. Take note of the best method to obtain listings in your BDA area, then spend 80% of your time on that.

Stick to the basics. Stay in touch with your database. Consistently speaking with your clients will lead to market appraisal requests, resulting in listings and sales over time.

Incidentally, as a basic calculation, an agent who would like to achieve four sales per month would need to aim to list circa fifteen properties over a 3-month period, based on an average of 80% of properties being sold.

Newcomers to the industry have this romantic notion that all they will be doing is showing buyers through beautiful places all day long. The reality is, showing properties is just 20% of the work. The other 80% is prospecting, dealing with a constant stream of information, death by email, and countless phone calls and meetings. Not to mention putting out fires with banks, valuers, solicitors, buyers, sellers, tenants, property managers, other agents, and marketing companies.

Employing a personal assistant or outsourcing some work can assist with the huge workload. An assistant can step in to deal with the day-to-day administration, conduct inspections and follow up with clients. Nonetheless, working with a PA can be a two-edged sword, taking the cream right off the top of your income, and putting on extra pressure to achieve an additional X number of sales. Training staff is time consuming; values may not align; and all the other issues that come with managing staff may come to the surface.

When I compare notes on the PA option with other agents, we often end up having the same discussion. Find the right assistant and productivity goes up. Find the wrong one and you can burn money and be more stressed.

Support staff can get edgy when they see the big commissions roll in and believe they are worth more, ignoring the massive overheads of any small business with the continuous costs of office expenses, marketing, insurances, and IT systems. I believe a consultant who can step in and out of the role, with the business ups and downs, is a better fit.

Outsourcing for specific tasks has worked well for me over the years. A couple of services I would not do without are accounting and IT, as systems need to work 24/7. I am happy to pay as much as it takes to have the privilege of uninterrupted tech service, which I believe is non-negotiable for a professional business.

Flexibility and focus are key in the real estate life, where long hours, high-stress situations and huge workloads are the norm. You either love it or hate it! Still, if you're reading this book, chances are that you are one of the 80% of people I meet who toy with the idea of a career in real estate.

Knowledge

Gaining professional skills will give you the edge when in front of clients. Knowing values in your BDA extremely well will increase your confidence and make you more relaxed with prospective sellers, resulting in first-class listing presentations and higher rates of listings.

The REIQ introduced a non-compulsory accreditation system encouraging agents to participate in further education. This is a step in the right direction for our industry as agents should become more professional and respected in the public eye and play nicer. Accredited agents can use this badge as an influential tool in their listing repertoire.

Information is king! Subscriptions to industry newsletters as well as those from solicitors, valuation companies and quantity surveyors are a perfect way to stay informed. Industry functions with some of these companies, and particularly with the REIQ, offer invaluable opportunities to be well-informed of current market conditions and legislation.

Professional development programs can add to your expertise and offer credibility and a point of difference. During my career I have made it a point to add qualifications where I thought they were applicable. This includes the diploma as a financial advisor, which proved to be very useful with off-the-plan project sales.

Clients expect agents to be across the local property market as well as have expert know-how. Learning new skills and developing new capabilities through continual professional development keeps the door open to successes.

# My biggest motivation? Just to keep challenging myself. I see life almost like one long University education that I never had—every day I'm learning something new.'

– Richard Branson, Virgin Group

Early on in my career one of my managers exclaimed, 'Hannah you are like a bullterrier with a bone!' I took that as a compliment... rruff!

I remember being daunted by what seemed an impossible mountain to climb. But this didn't deter me, as I desired to become a real estate agent so badly. I regularly stayed in the office late to follow up on thousands of leads. I received lots of rejections, but at the same time gained tons of experience, and in turn, shortened that steep learning curve and climbed that mountain persistently to the top.

One of Eleanor Roosevelt's quotes inspires newcomers to real estate: 'You gain strength, courage and confidence by every experience in which you really stop, to look fear in the face. You must do the thing you think you cannot do.'

From my experience and conviction, a successful real estate agent ticks most of the following boxes:

- ✓ Never-give-up attitude
- ✓ Self-starter with a vision
- ✓ Hard worker
- ✓ Passion for people
- ✓ Charismatic
- ✓ Highest integrity
- ✓ Entrepreneurial mindset
- ✓ Problem solver

✓ OCD and proud of it
✓ Lifelong learner

So, to all the newbies out there, act like you're already successful. Whilst there is no silver bullet, a fulfilling career in real estate is definitely achievable with hard work. It means simply starting the day with the right mindset, some physical exercise, and a good to-do list.

Consistency is the key to prioritising productive habits and following the 80/20 rule.

Importantly TAKE ACTION (right now)! Dig deep with every inch of your willpower and ignore the pessimists around you. Persistence is the key ingredient. Don't let go of that bone! Sear two letters into your soul: HS. Hard work, and Strength.

And don't forget, the soft touch is as powerful as the push!

"

# If it were easy, everybody would do it. Hard is what makes it great.'

– Tom Hanks

# 3 Business GROWTH is made of this (2004-2022)

# Chapter Nineteen

# Start of Business

Why start my own business?

Eight frenetic years in property! I had bounced between various sales positions and project management roles and my real estate career was in full swing. Yet as a female employee, I felt invisible. There was something niggling away in the back of my mind. I couldn't ignore the fact any longer that I had been repeatedly bypassed for top jobs.

Acutely aware that I had a 'fat chance' of advancing from my current position into an executive role, I was keen to find another way to achieve more.

With a burning desire to be once again in control of my own destiny, I plucked up all my courage and started my own business, HS Brisbane Property, in 2004. This was a huge challenge in every respect, from sourcing funding to surviving the start-up mode, and dealing with my own nagging voice: 'Will I be able to show the men around me that I am as competent as them?'

That was, of course, before I reminded myself to trust my own powers and emotions—the most powerful traits women will ever need for success. I fine-tuned my attitude and my voice to 'Don't worry about the competition' and 'Let's do it my way'!

Even today, twenty years later, gender inequality still exists, as highlighted in an article by Jessica Bahr (SBS News, 12 December 2022). The key points from the report were:

- The gender pay gap has stalled at 22.8% in 2022, with women earning $26,596 per annum less than men on average.
- The Workplace Gender Equality Agency says it's the first time the pay gap has stalled.
- The Global Gender Gap Report 2022 ranked Australia 43rd in the world for gender equality.

"

# Women who seek to be equal with men lack ambition.'

– sometimes attributed to Marilyn Monroe. True source unknown.

The gender pay gap encompasses not only women being paid less than men for similar roles, but women filling fewer positions in leadership roles and on boards, or stepping back from full-time work for family reasons.

Many businesses pay lip service to diversity. Typically, though, people are utterly unaware of their own prejudices, and workplaces discriminate against women due to unconscious bias.

Wikipedia describes unconscious bias, or implicit bias, as 'The underlying attitudes and stereotypes that people unconsciously attribute to another person or group of people that affect how they understand and engage with them'.

Best-selling author Malcolm Gladwell's book, *Blink*, discusses a fascinating test that uncovers a person's hidden biases. The Implicit Association Test (IAT) developed by professors from Harvard, the University of Virginia and the University of Washington, measures the two levels that all people operate within—the conscious and the unconscious.[3] Malcolm says the conscious level includes 'the decisions we make deliberately and things that we're aware of. I chose to wear these clothes. I choose the books I read'.

The unconscious level can tell you more about a person's true feelings. 'There's another level below the surface, which is the kind of stuff that comes out, tumbles out before we have a chance to think about it. Our snap decisions. Our first impressions.' Malcolm says.[4]

Interestingly, research from Dr Virginia Mapedzahama PhD, of Diversity Australia, suggests that even when workplaces are committed to diversity, it needs to be managed better than is currently happening to effect real change.

Dr Mapedzahama says the main problem with diversity, equity and inclusion is that people tend to focus on diversity and forget about equity and inclusion. 'Diversity is just getting a lot of people to your workplace,' she says. 'Inclusion is making that diversity work. So, just because you've got people in your workplace [who] are diverse, it doesn't necessarily mean that makes it inclusive. And, then, equity is just making sure that everybody has access to the same resources.' (Source: ABC News / Diversity Council Australia)

I am sure Dr Mapedzahama's deeper analogy of the diversity conundrum does resonate with women in workplaces all around Australia.

Several organisations aim to address gender inequity, both in Australia and internationally. Diversity Council Australia (DCA) promotes programs to create awareness of unconscious bias. Others are the Workplace Gender Equality Agency (WGEA), Women in Mining and Resources Queensland (WIMARQ), Women in

Mining and Resources Western Australia (WIMWA), International Women's Development Agency (IWDA), Australian Human Rights Commission (AHRC) and the Australian Gender Equality Council (AGEC).

## What was it like setting up my own business as a woman?

Prior to commencing my business, I had checked in with a government department's Small Business Advisory service for tips on how to start my business. When I left the (free) appointment, I was in a daze, clutching a compliance booklet, statistics, and some other mostly impracticable information. It was a soul-destroying experience and at the same time a light bulb moment!

Clearly, if I wanted to start my own business, I must take a leap of faith and just do it. I realised no one would hold my hand. I had to quit worrying about failure and throw caution to the wind. There would never be a perfect moment: I had to start now!

There is a strong correlation between going on an adventure and starting up a business. Claire Wyatt, a young adventurer from England, who I met while travelling around Australia in 2023, says: 'While I take preparation seriously, I also believe that the biggest hurdle in any adventure is simply starting. Many adventures never happen because people struggle to take that first step. You can talk about your plans for years, but it's putting them into action that can be the tough part. My decision to embark on a 16,000 km solo bike tour across Australia was very last-minute. I had a one-year visa and a flexible remote job, which I knew I could balance with cycling. Once I made up my mind, I didn't look back.'

It was game on for me once again, when my venture into real estate began. The first few months were beyond exciting as I travelled a rocky road – and not the delicious chocolate kind. Investing tens of thousands of dollars in equipment and systems felt overwhelming and confusing. Setting up and managing the business conflicted with my urge to just get out there, win clients and make it happen as I went.

Challenges ranged from employing the right support staff to choosing which market segment to specialise in. I weighed up my options. High-end properties in the inner city were in a highly contested segment of the market, already well-served by established agents and I was not keen to join them in that lion's den.

After careful consideration, I decided to focus my energy and resources on medium-priced properties. This was a good decision as there was plenty of product available, with over 7000 pieces of stock in the Brisbane CBD alone, and more in the surrounding inner city suburbs.

"

# I learned to always take on things I'd never done before. Growth and comfort do not coexist.'

– Virginia Romerty

## The money

Then there was organising business banking and a trust account. Instead of using one of the big-four banks, I found dealing with a smaller customer-centric bank easiest. Especially as I had to justify the fact that I was a female applicant in real estate, both factors commonly perceived as high risk by financial institutions.

Paying no mind to that, I pushed for the highest line of credit possible! Establishing an overdraft facility was very useful for me, as the commissions I received fluctuated wildly from month to month. It was also a circuit breaker in property downturns. Worries about cash flow can be detrimental to any business performance in slow periods, and have been known to cause great stress to real estate agents who are not careful with their money in the good times.

## Business plan

I took my finance application seriously and compiled loads of supporting documents, including the Big One. The business plan is a challenging exercise that details your ability to generate leads, and outlines sales targets, timelines, and budgets. It's the framework for the responsibilities that come with running your own business and it sure makes you realise it's actually happening. It was a practical strategy that transformed my aspirations into reality.

A business plan also shines a light on the strengths and weaknesses of the potential enterprise, revealed by a SWOT analysis. SWOT is an acronym for the four components the exercise examines:

- *Strengths*: characteristics of the business or project that give it an advantage over others
- *Weaknesses*: characteristics that place the business or project at a disadvantage relative to others
- *Opportunities*: elements in the environment that the business or project could exploit to its advantage
- *Threats*: elements in the environment that could cause trouble for the business or project[5]

Some of the entries in my original SWOT analysis were:

*Strengths*

- Boutique business with high flexibility, personalised service and responsiveness.
- Experienced operator in the real estate sector with sound market knowledge
- Good connections within the industry and with potentials
- Highly regarded in the marketplace, and positive testimonials

*Weaknesses*

- Limited staff could mean diminished customer service when business grows too quickly
- Home office versus competing with well-established offices
- No brand identity
- No rent roll resulting in losing business to offices who manage the properties

*Opportunities*

- No rent roll provides opportunity to establish strong referral relationships with on-site managers of apartment buildings and property managers without a sales department
- Personal contacts and sphere of influence
- Listing incentives for clients and affiliates
- Competitive commission structures and marketing packages

*Threats*

- Established agencies with high competition for high-end properties
- Home office versus shop front office
- Low inventory of listings due to start-up

On reflection, some of my fears were unsubstantiated. For example, when investors were selling their properties, they often did not like to engage the sales team from their property management office. Either they were disenchanted with their services or didn't like to deal with their sales department for other reasons.

The reality is that the roles of property managers and sales agents are generally conflicting—one strives to build long-term income by managing a property for a client, while the other strives for fast income for selling a client's property—and they don't communicate well. This results in a substantial loss in opportunities for listings and surprisingly, even some top offices do this badly. To keep sales business in-house, offices need to devise meaningful incentive schemes for property managers and close the gaps in appropriate training for the sales team.

Property managers are highly stressed due to their huge workloads and don't have the time or desire to recommend their sales team. They generally feel taken for granted and receive very little recognition. Sometimes kind words like 'You're doing amazing work' and 'What can we do to improve systems?' would make all the difference. Not surprisingly, there is high staff turnover which adds to the problem.

My business benefitted greatly when I established real connections with property management staff. As a rule, I made all meetings fun and memorable without pushing my agenda, and showed my appreciation with a big 'Thank you' and small tokens of gratitude like scratchies, chocolates, fresh coffee and pastries. The key is to build strong relationships, as it's always about how you make people feel.

There is no denying that creating a business plan is an arduous but beneficial task because it keeps your focus firmly on accomplishing short-term and long-term sales objectives. Its content needs to be revised regularly. For time-poor small business owners, this might be at six- or twelve-monthly intervals – or never. Only kidding! Not.

Creating a business plan and obtaining a line of credit were just two of the challenges to deal with, along with launching a business website in time, designing competitive marketing plans, and setting up a database for contacts' details and information, otherwise known as a customer relationship management (CRM) system.

## Systems

Setting up systems wisely is akin to choosing the right real estate office when starting out; both are extremely important to success. Once locked into a CRM system or IT structure it's nigh on impossible to change providers. The wrong choice results in loss of productivity and marketing opportunities, and additional expenditure.

I learned this the hard way once when my CRM system had been down for a few days. Losing patience, I asked the CRM specialist, 'Are you confident that you can fix it today?'

He replied, 'I don't know how!'

What.... #%!?

I want to stress the importance of researching the best options for your own IT, CRM, marketing, phone, and Internet provider companies. Don't engage the cheapest. I suggest you pay more for 24-hour/7-day service.

Ideally, everything will be ready to go prior to pressing the start button on your business, though there are always plenty of last-minute hiccups.

I found the following things to be pivotal to my success, and recommend them to anyone starting up a business:

1.  Find the best-fit IT company for the business, and word-of-mouth recommendations are usually the most reliable source for that. A good operator can save you sleepless nights when systems go down. Good IT support is a non-negotiable and money needs to be spent on this to keep the sales wheels turning.

2.  Choose the right customer relationship manage-
    ment software. Sounds boring? This is one of
    the most important tools for business success.
    Be aware of lock-in contracts and finer details
    when signing with one of the many providers.
    Once committed to a CRM system it will be a
    costly and onerous exercise to change.

3.  Engage a marketing agency. Branding is
    important to a point. People need to recognise
    you're in business. The budget you allocate for
    marketing depends on how big your ego is and
    how much money you're able to throw at it.

I have seen an agent with fabulous branding, a bril-
liantly designed business name, logo, website, and
classy office spend hundreds of thousands of dollars
to establish themselves, only to close the doors within
twelve months.

It seems to me sometimes the least efficient agents
have the highest marketing budgets. Did I just say
that? Don't get me wrong, branding is important, but
it needs to be backed up with high-quality service.

Starting a property company is very similar to starting
out as a real estate agent, with the addition of the
'managing' aspect and the additional red tape
required to run a small business. It entails a multitude
of costly business registrations, licensing, and, to a

lesser extent, the recommended industry-specific memberships, for example with the REIQ.

There are fees for company registration; accounting; and tax record keeping, including lodging a monthly (which means business is good) or quarterly business activity statement, known as a BAS. And don't forget the stringent regulation and associated costs for the biggie—trust accounting. (A trust account allows real estate and other agents to hold trust money on behalf of a client for an extended period, generally greater than 60 days.)

## Insurances

Additional expenses are the all-important insurances for business, including public liability and professional indemnity (PI). Both are non-negotiable when less than 1% of your clients or affiliates become unreasonable, or when you're being dragged into a situation by association.

The PI insurance became very useful three times over my 26 years in real estate. As anyone who has dealt with lawsuits will know, strong legal support in these cases will ensure you come through it emotionally and are able to continue with business throughout the drama.

I vividly recall one case which came about due to 'low fee disruptors', the do-it-yourself companies bursting onto the property scene. They promised clients easy transactions with huge savings in fees.

Several clients who had tried this option at the time came back to me, as it was too much of a tough gig. These wannabe sellers found out quickly that it's not all fun and games, and ultimately could cost more in additional marketing fees and potentially lower sales prices.

At the time, I signed a sales agreement for a two-bed inner city apartment. This client, who I will call Bruce, decided to list with me as we had previously met and connected.

Long story short, after a few weeks of marketing, Bruce became agitated and tried to move heaven and earth to get out of the agreement. It was all a bit strange. To top it off, he demanded his upfront marketing monies back, which was a measly $500 at the time and, of course, already spent, plus more, and eventually threatened me with legal action.

In a possible claim situation, it is important to immediately notify the PI insurer of a potential problem. By the way, this in turn can impact the PI insurance policy later regarding access fees and the seven-year run-off cover, which continues to provide cover for allegations of professional negligence after you're no longer practicing or have retired. In a nutshell, any claims may attract a higher one-off fee, i.e., an access fee; plus the insurer could demand extra payment for the run-off cover which would otherwise be free of charge.

Bruce unsuccessfully complained to the REIQ, the Office of Fair Trading, and anyone who would listen, but he had no case. The sales agreement was watertight, but the whole thing was upsetting all the same.

While we're on the subject, if a real estate agent only knows one thing, it would be how to fill in a Property Occupations Form 6 sales agreement correctly.

Firstly, it's prudent to be able to answer any of your clients' questions regarding this document. Explaining things well alleviates any concerns some anxious sellers may have and ensures the signing goes smoothly.

Secondly, solicitors regularly check these documents for errors and help clients get out of paying commissions. Thankfully, this has not happened to me, but apparently it's a regular occurrence.

It was hugely important to me to stay up to date with legislative changes and I ensured I squeezed time out of my busy schedule to regularly attend further development seminars with the REIQ.

But back to Bruce baby. I did let him out of the sales agreement, which I had offered to do right from the beginning of the saga. It only dragged on because he also demanded a refund for the $500 marketing fee.

True to form, shortly after he tried to sell his property through a DIY company and couldn't sell it. 'Dummkopf'! Twelve months on, he was audacious enough to ask me again if I would sell the property for him. I respectfully declined. WTH! The property was eventually sold below the price I had achieved for a similar unit in the same building.

## Licenses and registrations

In the real estate business, there is risk of 'death by licensing and membership costs' for both the company and the agent personally. Typical licenses and registration requirements are:

- Australian Business Register - all businesses require an Australian Business Number (ABN)
- Australian Securities & Investments Commission (ASIC) – Company & Business Registrations
- Office of Fair Trading (OFT) – Real estate licences both company and personal, and Trust Accounting
- Australian Tax Office (ATO) – Tax File Number registrations for both company and personal

- Real Estate Institute of Queensland (REIQ) – Membership for both corporate and personal
- Workcover QLD policy – registration required when employing staff

This involves filling in a huge amount of paperwork, including compliance documents, and walking a tightrope between being a good small business owner and going to jail.

Yes, I once received a letter threatening me with a huge fine or two years in jail as my accountant at the time missed lodging a trust account report by the due date. Lovely!

By and large, small business owners have to constantly jump through hoops, keeping government agencies busy. This saps enormous amounts of time, productivity suffers, and it takes energy away from what small business owners do best.

Building a business from scratch took all of my strength of character and determination to show myself what I was made of. The freedom to make decisions as I pleased was both exhilarating and frightening.

Through all the trials and errors, it was important to have the moral support of my family. Reminiscing with Mr Bigg recently, he told me that he knew I would not let it fail. How did I make it happen?

"

# Challenges give you wings Hannah, and you were always a bit of a rebel going your own way.'

- German friend, Usi

# Chapter Twenty

# Referral Business

In May 2004 I was ready to launch my business. My home office was complete with the systems I needed, and support dog Charlie in a cosy basket with a brown teddy bear under my desk: the office was buzzing. Two support staff and I were strategising our moves. We were all highly motivated and fired up to jump into action and start generating leads.

The plan of attack was to focus on obtaining listings as quickly as possible through referral opportunities and various marketing activities. Once a few properties are signed up for sale, that in turn creates more opportunities and kick-starts the business.

Simply put, this means 'find vendors wanting to sell property, then find suitable buyers and bring parties together resulting in successful sales.' In reality, after years of experience in real estate, I learned the basic formula is actually 'secure *saleable* properties and buyers will come'.

## Referral opportunities

*Referrals from on-site managers*

Whilst my assistants were busy in the office putting our strategy into action, I was on the road prospecting, meeting up with mortgage brokers, solicitors, and potential clients. Most of my time though was spent visiting inner city apartment buildings to introduce myself to as many property managers as possible. I was familiar with some of these unit blocks already, as I had sold them off the plan years earlier.

Business card and chocolates in hand, it was a numbers game. There were lots of rejections, which I expected and dismissed as I knew it would bring me one step closer to a 'YES'.

**"**

# You can have it all. Just not all at once.'

– Oprah Winfrey, media proprietor & personality

Some managers were already referring to a particular agency or were conducting sales themselves. Still, a few of them thought collaborating with me was of benefit for broader marketing, to show their clients that they were actively working on selling the property. The commission split would be typically less, however the exposure gained to the building would be priceless.

Fortunately, most rental agents didn't really enjoy selling. They were time poor or didn't want to pay the overheads for setting up the sales side of the business and found it easiest to just collect the referral fees.

My business card stated a referral incentive of a $500 Coles Myer gift card on the reverse side. Additionally, I would also offer a percentage of the sales commission, if I perceived the properties as quality listings.

These were properties where sellers had reasonable price expectations and there were no obvious issues. For example, a long tenancy lease on a property excludes owner-occupiers from buying, so can reduce the buyer pool to 40-50%, which then increases the time it takes to sell the property. Other impediments are requirements for major repairs or disputes over ownership, title, and mortgage issues.

I hit the jackpot when I met up with Carol, a manager in one of the inner-city serviced apartment buildings I visited. We had a lovely meeting and hit it off straight

Never take no personally. Sometimes people tell you no for a reason that has nothing to do with you. You must keep going.'

– Sofia Vergara

away. Before I left, Carol mentioned that one of her investors from New South Wales was thinking of selling his two properties. She told me she would be in touch with me the following week when she had heard back from them.

I was on tenterhooks, but didn't have to wait long, as a few days later Carol was in touch with the good news. She provided me with the seller's details, a lovely gentleman from interstate, who trusted her recommendation. Throughout the marketing process, Carol assisted me greatly with access to the units, as it was of course also in her best interest to affect a sale quickly. She even showed a couple of clients the property, to save me time.

A word of caution – by law, only employees of the company who possess a sales license or fully licensed agents are allowed to conduct inspections. This is not strictly monitored, still I never dared to cross that line. It is something to be mindful of!

It was a real boost to my confidence when I promptly sold both properties in the first months of business. Carol and I continued our relationship, with several other transactions over time.

Even after she had resigned, I continued listing properties in the building as potential sellers would get in touch after noticing our sales successes online.

We would also make sales from word-of-mouth recommendations from residents in the building.

The same process applied with other unit blocks where I started dominating sales. Once I gained a foothold, business would continue even after the referring property manager had left. Though I did appreciate the help and ease of doing business with them, it was a bonus not having to pay the referral fees.

*Word-of-mouth referrals*

The best referrals of all are from existing happy clients. As we got into the mechanics of the business, we designed systems to help us provide consistently superior service. We aspired to ensure the same standard for each sale and personalise the process by adding personal touches into the mix.

We created checklists for marketing presentations, listing procedures and contract administration. These procedures were documented in our HS Brisbane Property manual – an important document for easy reference and for new staff to learn the systems quickly.

Super focused, we did not want anything to go amiss. When, on the odd occasion something did go wrong, we apologised and fixed it. We then refined our systems for best practice and made our business run even more efficiently.

"

Be an example. Are you prompt? Are you professional? Are you engaged? As sales leaders, we have to set the bar high for ourselves as well as our teams.'

— Lori Richardson

Our motto was to under promise and over deliver. We did things differently. As a boutique business, we could be flexible with out-of-hours appointments and twilight inspections. We had the ability to be extremely responsive. Providing our clients with immediate attention was key, whether that meant answering phone calls and emails promptly, 24/7, or being on time and present for the client in one-on-one meetings.

It made people feel important and valued, and built our reputation. Other personalised services we provided included picking up interstate buyers from their accommodation for property viewings, assisting tenants with relocations, or freshening up a messy rental property.

We conscientiously ensured we made each transaction as easy as possible for everyone involved, and meticulously took care of the small details. Our aim was to build our brand quickly and establish a word-of-mouth business that resulted in enjoyable and rewarding relationships and, in the long-term, saved us big marketing dollars.

# Chapter Twenty-One

# Marketing

A considerable part of a real estate agents training is spent on learning how to convince a seller to part with as much of their advertising monies as possible. The argument is that the higher the marketing expenditure on a property for sale, the higher the price achieved in the shortest possible time will be, equally growing a real estate agent's profile and profiting online advertising portals.

Vendor-paid advertising (VPA), i.e., the dollar amount the agent requests from the seller, is usually 2-3% of the value of the property. The appropriate sum depends heavily on the type of property, the urgency of sale and the prevailing market conditions.

Arguably, an exclusive million-dollar property requires a higher marketing budget for greater reach, as the buyer pool is smaller for this type of product. Additionally, buyers psychologically associate a larger advertisement with a more exclusive property and a higher price. The reality is that larger advertisements, for various reasons, may not necessarily produce a better outcome.

Operating in a buyer's market may call for a more comprehensive marketing program so the property gets noticed when there is significant oversupply.

What is the ideal formula when it comes to marketing budgets? As a boutique business, I subscribed to the philosophy of finding a happy middle ground for our clients—fair and economical and just the right amount of exposure to reach the target audience, without breaking my seller's bank.

Weekly reviews of our marketing efforts ensured we reached the appropriate number of buyers. If we didn't, we had the flexibility to change the marketing to attract more enquiries.

In the real estate world, there are infinite ways to market a property, from old-style print advertising to the changing world of artificial intelligence (AI). Agencies need to stay up-to-date and frequently fine-tune their marketing efforts by reviewing and measuring the results for all strategies used in the pursuit of lead generation, growing the company's database, referrals, brand awareness and, of course, selling individual properties.

The following four marketing methods worked for us in our boutique business, promoting our property listings and successively our brand through sales results:

1. CRM database marketing – phone messaging, e-bulletins, mailouts
2. Traditional advertising methods – direct mail & print advertisements
3. Online marketing via
   - real estate portals: domain.com, realestate.com, homely.com, homesales.com.au, property.com.au
   - social media campaigns: Facebook, Instagram (owned by Facebook), LinkedIn, Twitter
   - search engine and pay per click (PPC) ads: Google, Gmail display and text ads, YouTube
4. Active marketing – open houses, signage, marketing specials like seasonal offers and 'no sale no cost to seller' offers, networking

## 1. CRM database marketing

I have already mentioned the importance of a robust and useful customer relationship management (CRM) system in business. The most important skill for a real estate agent, then, is to use that system effectively. A sound CRM is one of the most fundamental tools for client relationships, lead generation and productivity. Staying in touch with clients in a meaningful way is the key to a successful real estate business.

Managing a CRM correctly is an arduous task, but a necessary one. All contacts need to be entered promptly and appropriately, then followed up with an email to start the relationship but also to ensure the address provided is correct.

All client entries are stored and categorised in the CRM in an organised fashion.

For example, a new buyer entry would look like this:

- ✓ Name, address, email, phone contact
- ✓ 'Buyer A'
- ✓ Date of entry
- ✓ Price range for purchase
- ✓ Property they enquired about
- ✓ Source of lead
- ✓ Notes of conversation
- ✓ Follow-up call scheduled

This list can be expanded, but precise condensed categories are better for ease of managing contacts and the database. The KISS principle (keep it simple stupid) is best!

When listing new or off-market properties, the data bank can be effectively used to search for buyers in the appropriate price range and they can be contacted straight away via an e-bulletin or phone call.

Regular CRM reports reveal where leads are generated, and whether marketing dollars are being spent in the right areas.

A CRM assists in creating authentic relationships by recording the outcomes of conversations with clients. Notes can be made on the system about the timing for selling a property or revisiting a buyer when they are ready to make a move. The more detail the better. This could include details about the property in question, or buyers' requirements and certain circumstances like 'kids moving out of home' or 'a visit to Brisbane in X month'.

Here are the main reasons why a high-functioning database is useful for a real estate office:

- Organised contact list for phone, email and direct mail
- Systematised listing processes including records of current sellers for weekly feedback letters
- Measurable data to establish source of buyers and sellers and check that marketing monies are spent efficiently

"

# Life is too complicated not to be orderly.'

– Martha Stewart

- Updating contact details and purchase or sales information, plus scheduling follow-up calls
- Staying in touch with potential sellers for listings
- Search criteria option of buyers for new listings and off-market sales alerts
- Various email and mailout promotions
- Reports on effectiveness of email marketing campaigns
- Analysis and review of work processes
- Function to collect emails from clients subscribing through the company website
- Managing sales processes including contract administration

The most beneficial use of our database was emailing informative weekly (without fail) e-bulletins to 'our family of 20,000+ clients', which created long-term loyalty.

Frequently clients would approach me and excitedly exclaim, 'Hannah, it's me, George! You have been writing to me every week for over 10 years!'

'Hello George, of course. How are you?' Smile.

In my opinion, regular newsletters featuring the latest listings, blog posts and relevant information are one of the best ways for real estate companies to market their business and create a following.

Keeping a well-oiled data base, communicating often, and nurturing clients are vital.

## 2. Traditional advertising methods

*Direct mail advertising*

Marketing gurus will have you believe you need 'this' and 'that' social media platform – and online gimmicks. Sure, that may be fine as a supplement to your core marketing strategy but in my view won't be entirely effective until all the baby boomers (born 1946-1964) have handed their keys to the millennials (born 1981-1996). Right now, you still can't go past traditional mailouts to a carefully curated database for success in most real estate markets.

Direct mail is an important marketing tool and, guess what, unlike fleeting email bulletins, prospective sellers keep these informative letters on file, especially once they start either thinking about selling, or discussing values or investment options with their family or accountants.

Any marketing material sent to the database must stand out from the crowd. Consistency is key and these mailouts need to occur at least three to four times a year to strengthen customer relationships. Incidentally, many agents stopped posting letters to their database of contacts when the cost of stamps reached $1, but

I maintained this important connection, and I am confident it brought about positive results. (In 2023, the cost of standard letter postage is now $1.20.)

A word of caution regarding direct mail marketing. Check whether your business is regulated by the privacy laws of the Privacy Act 1988. Whilst these mailouts are part of the basic ABC of real estate, it becomes unpleasant when recipients have not been properly subscribed.

It's critical to keep track of response rates for all advertising activities and mark them against clients on your CRM system. This ensures monies are spent effectively, assisting with future marketing planning and ultimately creating more leads and increased sales.

Updating client entries when letters are returned saves money in subsequent mailouts. That is also where modern online data providers like CoreLogic become useful, as you can use them to check the ownership of a property in your mailing list. If the property changed hands, then the CRM entry needs to be updated.

Incidentally, a subscription to an online data provider is a must-have. CoreLogic and various other data companies are invaluable for the ease of accessing accurate market appraisals, conducting various sales research activities, doing business analyses, and importantly, making you look good in front of clients.

Online data portals have come a long way regarding the accuracy of data, although every now and then some of the attributes of properties need correcting, A little bias showing here, but I am now a big fan of CoreLogic's services and agree whole-heartedly with their following (unsponsored) product statement:

*'CoreLogic's real estate solutions provide powerful insights into the market, to help you become the local property expert. Our market-leading data and analytical tools, which cover approximately 98% of the property market, can help you make better informed decisions and grow your business. With valuable insights delivered at each stage of the property lifecycle, we can help you keep your clients engaged and informed at every step.'*

*Print advertisements*

Until about 2015, print marketing was the advertising tool of choice for maximising sales results. When I began my real estate career in 1996, it was all about advertising in various publications like The Courier Mail, Brisbane News and Local News.

Real estate offices would fight over the highest exposure, particularly in The Courier Mail. On Saturday mornings we waited in anticipation to see which real estate franchise had the most advertisements and would feature on the first page of the property insert.

Everything shifted with the World Wide Web and the ensuing digital revolution (1989-2005). The trend was away from print advertising, with buyers worldwide preferring to begin their property journey online.

By 2015 most real estate agents had stopped print advertisements. As a self-confessed 'real estate dinosaur', I chose to still place a prominent ad for all our Saturday open houses in the Courier Mail 'Open for Inspection' section until about mid-2016. None of my competitors were doing it, so the ad stood out. It was a cost-effective way to catch the buyers' eye and an easy tool for them to check inspection times, resulting in good interest.

Looking at the following statistics, it's indeed astonishing how technology has changed the way people search for their ideal property and how digitally connected we are.

According to DATAREPORTAL the stats for digital adoption in Australia in early 2023 show:

- There were 25.31 million internet users in Australia at the start of 2023, when internet penetration stood at 96.2 percent.
- Australia was home to 21.30 million social media users in January 2023, equating to 81.0 percent of the total population.
- A total of 32.71 million cellular mobile connections were active in Australia in early 2023, with

this figure equivalent to 124.3 percent of the total population.[6]

## 3. Online marketing

There are four distinct digital forms of marketing for real estate offices:

1. Property portals and company website
2. Search engine marketing
3. Social media campaigns
4. AI technologies

*Property portals and company website*

Over the last decade, real estate portals have burst onto the property scene. Before even stepping a foot into an open house, purchasers spend months surfing portals like domain.com, realestate.com, homely.com, homesales.com.au, property.com.au, and individual agency websites.

Advertisements on these portals are expensive, as sellers will tell you, and costs are ever increasing, and not just by the Consumer Price Index (CPI). Like trying to stay on top of a Google search (nigh impossible), it's a crazy system of keeping up with premium, top premium and uber top premium advertisements, year in, year out.

As I see it, the game goes like this. One leading agent includes the 'uber top premium' advertisements in their marketing proposals to sellers. Then when enough sellers have elected and paid for those high-priced ads, the agent's profile appears on the top of the portal search. Consequently, competitors in that same business development area (BDA) must follow suit. Some say 'that's business': I call it a vicious circle, with sellers paying the price, literally.

I have been fortunate to be able to buck this trend and stick with basic ads to save costs for my clients. My argument is that buyers usually search in their price range and budget. This narrows down the search result. Inevitably, they will come across an ad that is listed lower down on a page, i.e., below the premium ads. I believe that to be particularly true in a sellers' market, where there are limited properties being advertised.

Our business focused on medium-price CBD apartment sales. When advertising a large number of similar types of products, i.e., units with the same attributes, say 2-bed, 2-bath in the CBD, location was highly advantageous. We could direct buyers effortlessly between various property listings, which resulted in perpetual sales and consequent referrals.

There are typically a certain number of buyers looking for a property in the same area, or BDA, in any given three-to-four-month period. The right mix of

marketing—and each real estate office is different—
ensures that all these buyers are captured and matched
with the appropriate product. Incidentally, all agents
in a BDA area predictably work with the same buyers.

There is no question that property portals are critical
for any marketing strategy. But at the end of the day,
it's the experienced agent who engages with the right
buyer in a professional manner to extract the highest
price and a good result for the seller.

In addition to online portals, each real estate office
benefits from their own user-friendly website, ideally
complete with an informative regular blog. Blogging
shows clients your business is dependable and relatable,
and improves rankings on search engines and increases
traffic to the website.

*Search engine marketing*

A search engine marketing strategy is best left to the
professionals. It's a form of digital advertising, for
example pay-per-click (PPC), where the advertising
company receives a fee each time someone clicks on
an ad. Examples include Google, Gmail display and
text ads, and YouTube.

Search Engine Optimisation (SEO) is the process
of ensuring the company website appears on top of

a page when a consumer conducts a search for real estate in your BDA.

A professional marketing company may also take care of a business's online reputation by monitoring reviews.

*Social media campaigns*

The online marketing game becomes interesting with free or paid social media campaigns. This could include targeting a certain audience on Facebook, Instagram (owned by Facebook), LinkedIn, Pinterest and Twitter to build a social presence.

Online marketing needs to be facilitated by professional photographs, floor plans of properties, copy writing, videos and 3D home view tours. All expenditure should be in proportion to the value of the property.

*AI technologies*

Artificial intelligence (AI) is an emerging technology. Think Siri. The system relies on a computer's intelligence and progressive learning to assist with customer service and automated processes for administration, lead generation, and analysis of business results.

Some larger franchise offices are starting to implement AI. It can help with responding to web enquiries 24/7, for example, but as with any new technology, it's an expensive set up, and ongoing updates may prove costly. The AI agent will need ongoing training to be able to answer any enquiries professionally, or else conversations could go along these lines:

Client: 'Are you leading me up the garden path?'

AI agent: 'I can do that for you, Mate!'

4.  **Active marketing** – This includes open houses & signage, marketing specials, and networking

*Open houses & signage*

Conducting open houses (as many as possible) is one of the best ways to create activity and interest when selling properties. Appropriate signage put up in front of the property creates brand awareness.

Getting face-to-face with people, whether they are residents in the building of the property for sale, tenants, visitors from interstate, or indeed buyers, generates plenty of benefits.

Open houses create a buzz, build relationships and result in sales, which often do not occur on the day but through subsequent diligent follow-up. Even if the property on view is not suitable for a buyer, you may be able to direct them to another. Importantly, the sellers recognise and appreciate that the agent is working for them.

Open houses also offer an opportunity to conduct virtual inspections with interstate and overseas buyers. There needs to be a fair amount of trust between the agent and the buyer for sales to happen this way, and we sold multiple units in that fashion. It was a particularly good option during the challenging Covid times.

With experience, agents learn to qualify buyers and find out quickly who is in the best position to make a move. I often knew instinctively after a gentle inter-rogation—I mean chat—who I needed to focus on, of the multiple buyer groups attending. Answers like, 'I am moving to Brisbane next month and I am keen to find a property this weekend' are dead giveaways, versus 'Oh, I am looking for my son who is returning from overseas next year'.

A pet hate of mine during open houses were the negative buyers. As soon as they entered the apartment, they hunted down something to complain about. A bit like Pauline Hanson's famous line of 'I don't like it'.

This negativity is detrimental to the general vibe of the open house and influences other buyers who may be keen on the property but then have doubts because of the comments they hear.

This lack of enthusiasm needs to be dealt with swiftly by guiding the conversation to the positives of the property. I also typically would take this buyer aside and read them the riot act—I mean, ask them, politely, to discuss the aspects of the property later with me. In private. Outside.

Open houses are not just for collecting buyers' contact details. The agent needs to be like a performer on the stage—induce excitement about the property, provide tons of useful information, create fun and laughter, encourage people to relax and build lasting relationships.

*Marketing specials*

When the market turns to a sellers' market, it becomes a lot more difficult to list properties. We then would make the bold move of offering potential sellers a special 'No Sale No Cost' guarantee. The client would only pay for the marketing fees if the property was sold through us. This usually was a limited offer which resulted in lots of listings and sales.

We designed various specials for every season, including end-of-financial-year incentives: these offers provide a great reason to talk to the database and create activity.

*Networking*

Networking for some is fun and rewarding, however, it was never my thing. In fact, attending a networking function felt a bit 'plastic' to me. Most of my referrals came through existing happy clients. Still, I don't deny it can work well for some. Attending special networking groups with a focus on finance and investment, charities, and volunteer groups and similar, can be rewarding.

It also, of course, depends on which BDA an agent operates in. Local networking can mean being involved in the local community, and staying close to people, and being in the know when sales are coming up.

We did however establish a close relationship with, and sold several units to, a particular charity who used the properties as their raffle prizes. Similarly, we kept various buyer's agents informed with new listings.

There is no denying there is a strong correlation between marketing and referrals. However, as my business became more established, the reliance on traditional marketing methods diminished to some degree as our extensive database of satisfied clients did the heavy lifting. Principally, we received our leads by referrals. The marketing was there for additional exposure and, of course, to sell clients' properties.

Just a few months into the business in the extremely competitive market sector that was the Brisbane CBD, our marketing and referral strategies were bearing fruit. We consistently reached our listing and sales targets each month. Every sale was special to me, and I authentically connected with every one of our clients.

We really did put our heart and soul into each sale, from providing service beyond our client's expectation to personalised settlement gifts with special cards and referral requests.

We had followed our slogan, 'We promise to do the best for you—both personally and professionally', to a tee. As repeat business took off, with some properties being sold multiple times, we later refined our motto to 'Building enduring relationships'.

We continuously received positive testimonials and clients recommended us to their family and friends. Existing clients would often refuse our $500 Coles Myer gift card and say, 'Don't worry about it. I just like my friend to be looked after!'

Our business grew organically by satisfied sellers and buyers sharing the positive experience they had with HS Brisbane Property.

I didn't belong as a kid, and that always bothered me. If only I'd known that one day my differentness would be an asset, then my early life would have been much easier.'

—Bette Midler

"

# If your dreams do not scare you, they are not big enough.'

– Ellen Johnson Sirleaf, Liberian President (2006-2018) and first female head of state in an African country

# Chapter Twenty-Two

# Property Cycles & Covid

'Hannah what's the market doing?' Most Aussies are passionate about property and that's one question I get asked all of the time. My cheeky response, delivered with a broad smile: 'That depends; are you buying ... or selling?'

There is a distinct conflict of interest when agents answer this question about market conditions entirely truthfully. A negative response could result in lost opportunities for listings or sales, and any comment like 'Sales slowed down a bit this month' could cause a self-perpetuating downward spiral in the market.

Property markets can, and will, slow down, but some agents will claim, 'It's bloody fantastic', or, 'Unbelievable', before changing careers shortly afterwards. Even I must admit resorting to 'It's ticking along'—one of my favourite comments—or 'We had a really great month', and the occasional 'If I tell you, I will have to kill you'.

Whatever you do, choose your words wisely. It always amazes me when clients quote my comments many years later. 'Did I really say that?'

Property cycles track in four definite stages: upswing, boom, decline and stabilisation. Traditionally each phase lasts seven to eight years, depending on factors like supply and demand, the economy, consumer confidence, government policies, and the Reserve Bank of Australia's (fear-provoking) strategies on interest rates. Experienced real estate agents will do well in any property cycle, or at least survive until the market recovers.

Timing the market is almost impossible, but the good news is that properties tend to increase in value when held on a long-term basis.

Then there are some questions that are difficult to answer but asked regularly by potential sellers: 'Hannah, should I sell now or wait six or twelve months?' This is where ethical agents stand out. Honest feedback on the prevailing market conditions, current sales data and evidence for available similar properties currently listed for sale will assist the client to make an informed decision. There should always be a disclaimer that agents can't provide financial advice.

Property cycles have affected my business significantly, so much so that four out of the eighteen years in business resulted in absolute panic stations.

Starting out in May 2004, I worked extremely hard to establish myself and often felt overwhelmed in those early days. I remember my first year in business as the 'crying game'.

Then the fear of failing made way for riding a wave of success, and I increased sales year in year out, right up to dizzying heights in 2007, when the market peaked. I thought the party would never end and didn't pay much attention to market conditions. I was too wrapped up in the day-to-day running of my business. Anyway, who could have foreseen the Global Financial Crisis (GFC), which was in full swing in 2007-2008 and tanked my sales by 20%? In hindsight, that probably was still a good result.

## Downs

Simultaneously, life brewed up the perfect storm for me. The year of 2008 was a tumultuous time for my business, and equally for my relationship with Mr Bigg. And worst of all, my cat, Thursday, died. (Named Thursday, because that's the day I rescued the stray kitten.)

Yep, the breakup with Mr Bigg hurt like hell. I put on my best poker face and soldiered through it. That's what women do. Naturally, we remained friends and catch up now and then to check in on each other, reminiscing about the good times we had together, and comparing notes on anything to do with sales.

Then, in 2009, the Government added more pain for my business by removing the First Home Owners Grant. Despite this, and perhaps because of my heightened focus in 2008, I still achieved very good results.

## Ups

There were, of course, other positive factors as well. From 1998 to 2008, the number of two-salary households increased, as did real net national disposable incomes, going from $32,000 to $42,000 per year, on average (source Wikipedia). Lending standards were relaxed, and negative gearing was driving property investing.

Historically, residential property has done well in times of economic shock. Nevertheless, I learned the hard way that property markets, and in turn my business, are directly impacted by a multitude of major events.

The top four disruptors for my business were elections, anything to do with finance, government policies, and natural disasters.

- Firstly, the pesky state and federal elections: they come around far too quickly and regularly kill buyer activity, mostly due to uncertainty around how taxation rules might be impacted if there was to be a change in government.

- Secondly, rises in interest rates and stricter monetary policies, especially for lending criteria, can erode consumer confidence.

- Thirdly, expansionary and contractionary fiscal government policies influence buying decisions. Examples are capital gains and land tax rules, First Home Owner Grants, and stamp duty laws. Stimulus for migration drives up sales, as experienced in 2009 after the Government instigated a skilled migration program of 6000 places in 2007 to 2008.

- The fourth factor, natural disasters like bushfires and floods devastate people's lives and impact certain property markets. In contradiction, these events benefit the construction sector.

## Staying up to date

We learned to roll with the punches, and I ensured I was up to date with industry trends, economic data, and local and world events. I followed inflation, gross domestic product (GDP) reports, unemployment rates, consumer confidence levels, and the like.

I scanned industry-specific news, signed up for Google alerts and regularly jumped onto the Foreign Investment Review Board (FIRB) websites to check for changes. Affiliate accountants and solicitors assisted with advice on new laws and regulations.

I had mortgage brokers on tap in my database and kept a check on lending guidelines for different banks. I tracked which banks required what level of loan-to-value ratio (LVR)—the percentage of a loan compared to the value of the property. Most banks' benchmark is 80%, requiring a 20% deposit, but some demand a 30% deposit. In practice, that means a $90,000 deposit for a $300,000 property purchase.

First home buyers in particular struggle with that level of cash prerequisite and consequently miss out on the Australian dream of owning a home.

Other important requirements to stay on top of are lending rules for serviced apartments because in the Brisbane CBD most high-rise buildings are not all true owner-occupied places, and share a component of the floor space with serviced apartment (hotel) operators.

Higher deposit requirements for investors, and a bank's existing lending exposure to a building also play a role in buyers being able to obtain finance. Bank guidelines change frequently. Unfortunately, it seems like rules are set by head offices not in Queensland, but in other States, with a one-size-fits-all mentality.

In the industry, the most nail-biting data comes from the 'Big Kahuna', the chief of the Reserve Bank of Australia, who announces the RBA cash rate on the first Tuesday of every month. An increase in the cash rate most certainly leads to higher interest rates for mortgages and puts a dent in consumer confidence, generally resulting in a drop in sales.

I like to share anything newsworthy and educational with my clients through newsletters and information flyers, especially about specific subjects like the First Home Owner Grant, taxation and deprecation rules, body corporate principles, and critical conveyancing and market facts.

Further professional development, like completing a Diploma in Financial Advising in 2003, turned out to give me a real advantage. It gave me the edge over some of my competitors, affording me credibility and strengthening my reputation as an expert in my field. Naturally, I kept any discussions general and factual, as by law, real estate agents are not allowed to provide financial advice.

Essentially, keeping my finger on the pulse and being well informed helped me to build trust with clients, make better decisions in my business, and be in control of my destiny.

Traditionally, the price of a property in Australia had increased by around 0.5% per annum for a hundred years to 1990 (source Wikipedia). Things changed with the GFC in 2008 when values started rising faster, resulting in affordability issues due to a higher price-to-income ratio. This led to fears of a property bubble in the late 2000s, adding to the already scary situation.

Dealing with the challenges of running a small business and rolling with tumultuous market conditions at that time was almost all-absorbing for me. It then came as a bit of a surprise when, in 2009, a tennis game changed everything on a personal level.

I finally found my soul mate—let's call him 'Mr Even Bigger'. In a social tennis setting, I was paired up with him in a doubles game. From the outset, I made it very clear that if we lost, I would have to kill him. Naturally we won and he's been living in fear ever since.

Being English, he did not surrender straight away to this German woman. On another date, I invited him to my place for coffee. Never one for beating around the bush, I casually noted that he may be more comfortable in the bedroom, but years later, he still insists that he wasn't.

All jokes aside, it's amazing feeling deeply connected to my 'Treasure', sharing the same values and thinking the same thing at the exact same time!

## Down again

With renewed energy, I was ready to fight on when the RBA cooled the market by raising the cash rate three times in 2009 and again in 2010. If that was not concerning enough, the most frightening time came in 2010-2011 when I experienced a complete stand-still in my business.

Who can forget the disastrous floods on 12-13 January 2011, bringing Brisbane and the market to its knees. Yet, I was lucky again. Due to specialising in unit sales, I was still able to pull off a good year. People affected by the floods bought temporary accommodation while waiting for their properties to be repaired.

In 2012 and 2013, the Big Kahuna, the RBA's then-chief Glen Stevens, had cut interest rates from 3.25% to 2.5% and I worked my way through a few fabulous sales years.

Then wham, in 2016 the property market got smashed again! A federal election and APRA's 2015 introduction of a 10% growth limit for investments started to bite. Add to that a royal commission into lending and misconduct of financial institutions, and proposed changes to negative gearing in 2019. Investors dropped out of the market, and it was difficult for home buyers to obtain loans due to the credit squeeze.

When the property market turned challenging again from the end of 2017 to mid-2019, it was a matter of digging deep once again, staying focused, working hard, and drawing on my years of experience.

It meant tightening the belt by reducing business expenses and going back to the basic ABCs of real estate—contacting 100+ people from my database each day, and being super diligent with the follow-up. We phoned a mix of contacts from past appraisals, withdrawn properties, and buyers and sellers who had recently subscribed.

This led to increased sales proposals for clients. Never compromising our values, we would always make sure to quiz clients on the reason for selling, asking them, 'Have you spoken to your financial planner to check whether it's a good idea to liquidate this investment, as now may not the best time to sell?'

People need to sell for all sorts of reasons. If buying and selling in the same market, especially when upgrading, that's generally fine. We always suggested clients check with their accountant for their best option going forward.

## A sorry story of off-the-plan sales

From about 2005 onwards, the market gradually changed. Property prices increased for off-the-plan sales, but buyers were still sold on the idea that buying off the plan meant units would be worth more on settlement.

Cindy, a Melbourne buyer, purchased two properties off the plan in 2016 through an interstate agency. She paid around $700,000 for each and repeatedly contacted me, desperate to sell prior to settlement. Each time, I had to advise her that her losses would be too great.

Finance conditions had changed both in Australia and her country of origin, restricting monies to be taken out and restricting loans for investors, especially from overseas. This was coupled with extra taxes for overseas purchasers.

Changes to finance conditions or valuations of the property, i.e., values going down by the time the settlement comes along, are the risks when purchasing a property off the plan, closely followed by a change in personal circumstance, like divorce or loss of a job.

Cindy then called me again after settlement of the properties. I had to inform her that I believed the apartments were not worth $700,000 in the current market and if she was to sell, she would make a loss of about $150,000 on each, not taking the stamp duty and solicitor fees into account.

While I was speaking with her, I looked up sale prices on this new building. A similar unit had sold for $540,000. My dark suspicion was confirmed.

Of course, I would never keep her hopes up and list the properties first, then give her a reality check later, which is unfortunately a common practice of some real estate agents.

Fortunately, for every sad story there is a good one. Around the same time, I learned that another purchaser made a $400,000 profit on a sale in another CBD tower when on-selling an off-the-plan unit.

In 2017, property valuations for off-the-plan sales started to frequently come in under value. Compared to established property prices, off-the-plan sales appeared inflated. Banks only lend the amount of the valuation, not the contract price. This meant that on settlement of a new property, the purchasers could be faced with finding a substantial amount of extra funds.

The alternative for the buyer is not to settle, and kiss the 10% deposit goodbye. Plus, possibly be sued by the developer for the difference in the sale price when on-selling the property. This becomes a terribly distressing situation for a buyer, and I really do feel for them. Though, I can't blame the developer here, either. There are huge risks associated with off-the-plan building projects, and high risk does not always result in high rewards.

Despite limited interest from investors, between 2017 and mid-2019 there was still plenty of buyer activity from owner-occupiers. I just didn't have the appropriate properties for them!

## Diversification

Dr Spencer Johnson's book titled 'Who Moved my Cheese?' became my inspiration. It is a book about change. In a nutshell, when things dry up in one area of the business, one should diversify into other areas. That prompted me to look for new cheese.

I realised I had to be more proactive, rekindle that get-up-and-go spirit, and find new avenues to satisfy the specific demand from the owner-occupier market. I did my research and began to sell select off-the-plan properties on the city fringe.

Additionally, in 2018 I started consulting to another business that specialised in selling development sites. The company's values aligned with my own; things were either black or white – perfect. I very much enjoyed the work of assessing sites and dealing with builders and developers. Visionaries by nature, the clients were fun to deal with.

Builders are always forward looking. They like to hold on to their staff and contractors by keeping them engaged during lean times, even if a project reaps only a minor profit. Developers also habitually land-bank for future endeavours when the property market lifts. These are some of the reasons why development sites sales are not cyclical, compared to residential property sales.

A bonus was that most of the information for sites can be provided via email, and contracts are frequently signed electronically, site unseen. I must admit even I did not physically inspect a few of those properties I sold. Shhhh. I blame the amazing technology and resources I had at my fingertips and, of course, years of experience.

Typically, contracts for development sites had long lead times. Some settlements could be twelve months away, which didn't matter to me. Selling sites is not unlike residential sales, where lots of things can go pear-shaped prior to settlement. And of course, it's not quite as easy as I make it sound.

Most deals typically involve lots of tricky special conditions like 'subject to development approval' (DA), or 'subject to due diligence' (DD), which means the buyer can check all factors affecting a proposed development on the site or block of land for a month or, more often than not, six months before going ahead. This meant some contracts crashed, and tens of thousands of dollars in commissions went with them.

Nonetheless, successful sales presented nice pay cheques when they came to fruition.

Diversifying served me well during the challenging years from 2018 to 2021. It was beyond awesome supplementing earnings with sales from selling development sites, and this was especially true during 2020, when my anxiety level was high. And if you read on, you'll find out why.

"

# Obstacles are what you see when you take your eyes off your goals.'

– Justin Herald

## Things got weird in 2020

In late 2019, I started to see light at the end of the tunnel. Investors were returning to the market and just as my business began to do well, things got weird.

I listed a fabulous owner-occupied unit in one of the high-rise buildings. The sellers acted strange from the beginning. They were difficult to get hold of and were never present in the unit except on one occasion, before an inspection, when the husband opened the door to me wearing a mask. He told me he was extremely concerned about his dad who was quite ill with the flu.

After a few weeks, I sold the unit to an investor. At the same time, I became very sick with a strange chest infection which lasted for three months. I will never know whether the dreaded 'C' word and the sale of this unit had anything to do with it.

Then Covid arrived in earnest. I remember spending a weekend holiday on a New South Wales beach on 23 March 2020. Increasingly, there had been reports filtering through to Australia about a flu-like illness. It turned out to be my last trip to New South Wales for a couple of years.

As news reports from overseas about a pandemic intensified, I wondered what this would mean for my business. The situation escalated quickly, with the Queensland

Government imposing restrictions, including the first lockdown and border closure in March 2020. It was all a bit surreal, especially the risk of a fine for leaving home. By then, two million people globally had already died from the virus, and the threat was real.

I knew I had to stay calm. I reassured myself that I could handle it, and business would eventually be fine. And just as well, because the phone started ringing hot with concerned clients wondering what this would do to property prices.

What could I say? I listened intensely for the most part, and admitted we were in unchartered waters, adding that people will always need a place to live, and things will turn out just fine. As months dragged on, clients from the southern states started thinking of moving to Queensland just as soon as they could. That gave me hope.

In the meantime, I was in a frenzy, reducing my business expenses to an absolute minimum. First up was closing my trust account and handing that responsibility to the sellers' solicitors. This saved me a few thousand dollars a year in audits and bank fees, plus time. That would not have been an option if I operated a rent roll. I was no longer in control of the deposits, so the risk of not operating a trust account was losing commissions if the seller's solicitor failed to hand them on. Luckily, this never happened.

66

# Everything will be okay in the end. If it's not okay, it's not the end.'

– John Lennon

Next was reducing subscription costs for online marketing and data portals. There were lots of tears when I had to let support staff and marketing consultants go. Unsurprisingly, I did not enjoy letting people down one bit, and felt fatigued and mentally exhausted.

After the 'blitzkrieg' of cutting costs for the business and rearranging finances on a personal level, I started to feel more optimistic.

A few months into lockdowns, Mr Even Bigger casually mentioned, 'My work wants to know who of us would like to come back and work from the city office'.

Not missing a beat, I said, 'You do!' There can sometimes be too much of a good thing.

*    *    *

During my business career I had plenty of practice sticking it out through the tough times, testing my ability to survive and still enjoy a reasonable income. Covid was no different. The game plan was to stay in control. Incidentally, I was one of those toilet paper hoarders. Before judging me too harshly, listen to this—according to a scientific study published in the open access journal PLOS ONE, 'People who panic buy and hoard toilet paper score high in personality assessment for traits of conscientiousness'.

Whilst battening down the hatches, I was in the fortunate position that I had residual settlements for both my business and consulting coming in each month in the first half of 2020.

Interestingly, during those early months of the pandemic I also found out that I was unemployable. I had been applying for plenty of over-fifty jobs, without luck. This turned out to be a good thing as I stayed very focused on the business.

It's well documented that the property market is closely linked to the economy. When ensuing lockdowns hit, I was not surprised that business was unnervingly quiet until around June. Then the unexpected happened, and buyer enquiries progressively picked up. I didn't quite want to believe it at first, but there were flurries of activity and sales took off.

Some people decided to simplify their lives by moving into a unit; others wanted to cut costs; and interstate buyers were keen to purchase in readiness for a move to sunnier Brisbane. A few thought the sky was falling so they might as well sell up and retire, whilst others liquidated investments to make a sea or tree change.

Despite a lot of uncertainty in the economy, market Armageddon turned into a property boom no one could have foreseen. If anything, most economists expected a drop in property values by 20-30%.

Due to government stimulus programs, like JobKeeper, which helped prevent businesses from collapsing, early access to superannuation, spare cash reserves from a reduced lifestyle and no travel, and the whopper low interest rates, many were tempted into property. The market went crazy and sales skyrocketed, making 2021 the second-best year in my business journey.

Suddenly, sellers found themselves in the box seat. We achieved fantastic prices for them, as there were limited properties for sale. Many people were reluctant to make a move for various reasons, including having their grown children living back home during the pandemic.

As a rule, in real estate there is either a buyers' or sellers' market. I can't recall ever operating in a balanced marketplace, where equal numbers of people were looking to buy or sell. A sellers' market, like in 2021, happens when there are more buyers than active sellers, opposed to a buyers' market, where there are few buyers with plenty of properties for sale.

CoreLogic's data reveals that following the pandemic population surge, Greater Brisbane home values increased by more than 43% and hit a record high on 19 June 2022, soon after the Reserve Bank of Australia commenced its rate-tightening cycle. Enough said about that!

In the early months of 2022, Brisbane experienced another devastating flood. Despite that, we operated in a healthy property market with another exceptional and final year for HS Brisbane Property.

*    *    *

Why, then, did I close my business when 2023 promised to be even better for property in the Brisbane CBD?

In a nutshell, the stars aligned. My partner retired at the end of 2022, perfect timing for us to fulfill our dream for an unlimited travel adventure around Australia.

There was no denying I had mixed feelings, finishing on top of my game. With great trepidation that any addict would feel, I decided to let go of this wonderful business that is real estate!

IT'S NOT THE END

# A New Adventure

I hope I have inspired some of you to take the next step on an exciting property adventure. It's as simple as creating a business plan, researching funding and discovering the ideal niched business development area that ignites your passion!

Why not? If this German backpacker can do it, so can YOU!

What helped me thrive in business?

- My unfaltering belief in my own abilities
- My genuine desire to help my clients achieve best results
- Being proactive and showing initiative, no matter what comes at me
- Continuously investing in personal development
- Willingness to put in extra time and effort
- Being motivated to do better by setbacks
- Addressing issues quickly, and being accountable
- My ability to draw on mental strength when needed
- Always being guided by strong values

… and above all, standing out for applying the soft touch in the industry, rather than the usual push!

So, you have your business plan? Tick.

Ideal BDA? Tick.

Finances? Tick.

Sounds like you're in for a wild property ride!

\* \* \*

The reason I've been able to be so financially successful is my focus has never, ever for one minute been money.'

– Oprah Winfrey

What's next for me....

My next adventure is a trip over the rainbow, travelling around this amazing country with my Englishman for a year. As I conclude this book, we are in a VW campervan heading north with no plans, except to eventually swim with the whale sharks in Ningaloo Reef in NW Western Australia.

The overriding goal for me is to reconnect with nature and my true spirit, and discover a sense of awe, with tons of goosebumps.

I wish to reinvent myself on this journey. Develop a feeling of absolute freedom, knowing that anything is possible. Heighten my awareness and skills as a life coach, with focus on humility, kindness and sensitivity to really listen, motivating women to be stronger and to aim higher.

Just as I credit my book coach, Bev Ryan, (www.smart-womenpublish.com) with inspiring me to finish this book, I would like in turn to help women find their 'why' and achieve goals beyond their wildest dreams.

I love to help evoke greater change by coaching and empowering one woman at a time—not only a woman in real estate, but any woman who wants to live a life with purpose, joy and success.

## My commitment as a life coach to you

- Total listening, personalised care, and measurable success
- Creating easy-to-implement strategies together
- Your increased confidence and trust, for your best life

## Imagine the empowered YOU

- Discover your core needs, desires, uniqueness, and worth
- Develop your strength and power with confidence for rewarding relationships and career
- Take charge of your life beyond your wildest dreams

Please stay in touch at hannah@coachingforwomen.au or visit www.coachingforwomen.au to read my travel blogs and subscribe to my newsletter.

*To a stronger & higher you*
*Aufwiedersehen*
*Hannah*

Check Hannah's travel blogs at:
www.coachingforwomen.au/blog/

# References

[1] www.psychologytoday.com

[2] https://hbr.org/2011/04/building-resilience

[3] https://implicit.harvard.edu/implicit/Study?tid=-1

[4] https://www.oprah.com/oprahshow/overcoming-prejudice/13

[5] https://en.wikipedia.org/wiki/SWOT_analysis

[6] www.datareportal.com

# Other Resources

DiSC® assessment: www.discpersonalitytesting.com/free-disc-test

**Online property marketing sites:**

www.domain.com
www.realestate.com
www.homely.com
www.homesales.com.au
www.property.com.au

**Relevant government sites:**

Australian Business Register - all businesses require an Australian Business Number (ABN): www.business.gov.au/registrations/register-for-an-australian-business-number-abn

Australian Securities & Investments Commission (ASIC) – Company & Business Registrations: www.asic.gov.au/for-business/registering-a-business-name

Office of Fair Trading (OFT) – Real estate licences both company and personal, and Trust Accounting: www.qld.gov.au/law/fair-trading

Australian Tax Office (ATO) – Tax File number registrations for both company and personal: www.ato.gov.au/Business/Registration

**Real Estate Institutes: Professional associations for the real estate industry**

Real Estate Institute of Australia (REIA): www.reia.com.au
Real Estate Institute of Queensland (REIQ): www.reiq.com
Real Estate Institute of New South Wales (REINSW): www.reinsw.com.au
Real Estate Institute of Victoria (REIV): www.reiv.com.au
Real Estate Institute of Western Australia (REIWA): www.reiwa.com.au
Real Estate Institute of Northern Territory (REINT): www.reint.com.au
Real Estate Institute Of The Australian Capital Territory (REIACT): www.reiact.com.au

**Workcover: required registration
when employing staff**

Workcover Queensland:
www.worksafe.qld.gov.au/licensing-and-registra-
tions
Workcover New South Wales:
www.workcover.nsw.gov.au
WorkSafe Victoria: www.worksafe.vic.gov.au
WorkCover Western Australia:
www.workcover.wa.gov.au
NT WorkSafe: www.worksafe.nt.gov.au
WorkSafe ACT: www.worksafe.act.gov.au

# Acknowledgements

Sincere gratitude to my amazing partner, 'English Treasure'.

You're my rock and my real success. Your natural instincts for truth, your optimism, and your happy nature make my life 'wunderbar'.

Just sometimes you take too much pleasure in teasing me with the score of 2:0 and questioning me before every single vacation: 'Are we going to invade or going on a holiday?'

A special 'danke schoen' to my beautiful sister, Ingeborg, who has always been there for me and our family.

And huge thanks to Bev Ryan, my book coach from Smart Women Publish, for getting me to the finishing line. Now another adventure begins.

# About the Author

Hannah Schuhmann is a successful business owner and author, and now a coach who is committed to inspiring women to reach their highest potential in business and life.

Hannah has lived an adventurous life because she took control of her own decisions and destiny at a very early age, as her book, *Confessions of a Woman in Real Estate*, illustrates.

Hannah was Principal of HS Brisbane Property from 2004 to December 2022. She survived and thrived through tough times and good in a male-dominated environment by avoiding the 'dark side' of the industry and doing things her way, where her soft touch was often more powerful than their push. Her boutique real estate agency specialised in the Brisbane inner-city property market – primarily CBD apartments – and offered flexibility and individual marketing & service solutions.

Her passion now as an author and life coach is helping women in all vocations, but particularly real estate, to exhilarate and accelerate their careers.

She loves assisting her 'fellow sisters' to find their passion and achieve a fulfilling life where ANY AWESOME THING is possible.

Hannah invites you to join her here:
www.coachingforwomen.au

# Photo Collection

Hannah on her First Communion Day outside her home
in Lohr am Main, Bavaria, in Germany – 1970

Skiing the Swiss Alps while working there as an
Assistant Manager in a 5-star hotel – 1986

Backpacking and travelling outback Australia
by Greyhound bus – 1989

The VW Golf that financed Hannah's travels – 1989

Starting out in real estate in Brisbane, Queensland – 1997

Hannah in Coral Bay, Western Australia, travelling the
country again during her sabbatical – 2023

Milton Keynes UK
Ingram Content Group UK Ltd.
UKHW022214180823
426895UK00011B/65